125 best
Rotisserie
Oven
recipes

125 best
Rotisserie
Oven
recipes

Judith Finlayson

Robert
ROSE

For complete cataloguing information, see page 182.

Disclaimer
The recipes in this book have been carefully tested by our kitchen and our tasters. To the best of our knowledge, they are safe and nutritious for ordinary use and users. For those people with food or other allergies, or who have special food requirements or health issues, please read the suggested contents of each recipe carefully and determine whether or not they may create a problem for you. All recipes are used at the risk of the consumer. Consumers should always consult their rotisserie oven manufacturer's manual for recommended procedures and cooking times.

We cannot be responsible for any hazards, loss or damage that may occur as a result of any recipe use.

For those with special needs, allergies, requirements or health problems, in the event of any doubt, please contact your medical adviser prior to the use of any recipe.

Design & Production: PageWave Graphics Inc.
Editor: Carol Sherman
Recipe Testers: Jennifer MacKenzie and Audrey King
Copy Editor: Julia Armstrong
Photography: Mark T. Shapiro
Food Styling: Kate Bush
Prop Styling: Charlene Ericson
Illustrations: Kveta Jelinek

Cover image: Basic Rotisserie Chicken (page 17)

We acknowledge the financial support of the Government of Canada through the Book Publishing Industry Development Program (BPIDP) for our publishing activities.

Published by Robert Rose Inc.
120 Eglinton Avenue East, Suite 800, Toronto, Ontario, Canada M4P 1E2
Tel: (416) 322-6552 Fax: (416) 322-6936

Printed in Canada
1 2 3 4 5 6 7 8 9 FP 13 12 11 10 09 08 07 06 05

Contents

Acknowledgments

Although I am the author, many talented people worked diligently behind the scenes to produce this book. It's our fifth as a creative team, and the process keeps improving each time. Thank you to the group at PageWave Graphics — Andrew Smith, Joseph Gisini, Kevin Cockburn and Daniella Zanchetta — who do such a superb job of integrating all the visual elements with the text; Mark Shapiro for his beautiful photographs; food stylist Kate Bush for making my recipes look so delicious, and props stylist Charlene Ericson, who adds all the right flourishes; Jennifer MacKenzie and Audrey King for recipe testing; and, of course, editor Carol Sherman, who takes note of my oversights in the nicest way. Special thanks to my husband, Bob Dees, for his professional insight as well as his personal support.

Introduction

Unexpected guests and no time to fuss? Defrost a chicken, season and brush with oil, truss and load it onto the spit rods, and your work is virtually done. With a rotisserie oven, you just set the timer and check what's cooking from time to time, in the unlikely event that something has gone amiss. In about an hour, you'll be serving one of the most delicious roast chickens you've ever tasted. This basic formula also works for roasts of beef, pork and lamb, as well as many other foods.

Rotisserie cooking isn't new. Quite the contrary, in fact. Since the Stone Age, people have been cooking food on a stick, turning it occasionally to ensure even browning. Around the middle of the 15th century, expertise in the technique was identified, spawning the French term *rotisseur* to describe a purveyor of roast game and poultry.

What is new — and this goes a long way toward explaining the revival of interest in this ancient technique — is the relatively recent invention of the rotisserie oven, which makes the process extremely convenient. This stand-alone appliance contains a heating element and spit rods mounted on gear wheels that turn when powered by electricity. Depending on the model, rotisserie ovens also come with a dial or digital timer, some kind of tray for capturing the fat that melts during cooking, a basket for cooking smaller or more fragile foods, and a variety of optional accessories, such as kabob rods.

The units are available in several sizes (about the same size as microwave ovens). There are two main manufacturers: George Foreman, distributed by Salton; and Ronco, distributed by Popeil Inventions, Inc. De Longhi makes a convection oven with a rotisserie attachment, and some barbecues and ovens now come equipped with infrared burners for rotisserie cooking. Other manufacturers have their own versions in the works. Shop around and choose the model that suits you best. And get ready to enjoy some of the best home cooking you've ever done!

— Judith Finlayson

Using a Rotisserie Oven

There are numerous advantages to cooking meat in a rotisserie oven, not the least of which is that you don't need to be bothered with opening the oven door to brush a chicken or turkey with melted butter or oil. Not only does the meat baste itself, a significant quantity of fat drips off as it rotates, producing a healthier result. The stand-alone ovens cook with a moderate, even heat so that, assuming you've timed the cooking appropriately, meat is particularly juicy. Chickens and turkeys roast to crisp perfection, and vegetables and fish don't scorch, which can happen on the grill.

A rotisserie oven is a great tool for producing delicious oven-roasted food because it is so convenient. So long as the food is the appropriate size and correctly positioned, it cooks on its own and requires very little monitoring. The heat source is at the back of the oven, unlike a barbecue with a rotisserie attachment, which cooks using heat from burning coals below. This is significant because it means there are virtually no flare-ups. In a rotisserie oven, sparks will only fly if the food comes in contact with the heating element — a real no-no. If this happens, you should stop the machine immediately and reposition the food so that it does not touch any part of the oven.

Cooking in a Rotisserie Oven

Once you've mastered the art of positioning food on the spit rods, these appliances are easy to use. They are virtually foolproof, and even novice cooks can produce delectable results. However, the various models have different features. Before you begin to cook, thoroughly read the manual that came with your oven to make sure you understand how it operates and are completely aware of any safety precautions.

Not Brown Enough?

Because smaller cuts of meat cook for a shorter period of time, they may not be as browned as you like. If your machine has a "pause to sear" function, you can stop the rotation and position the meat directly in front of the heating element for a few minutes to intensify browning.

A Typical Rotisserie Oven

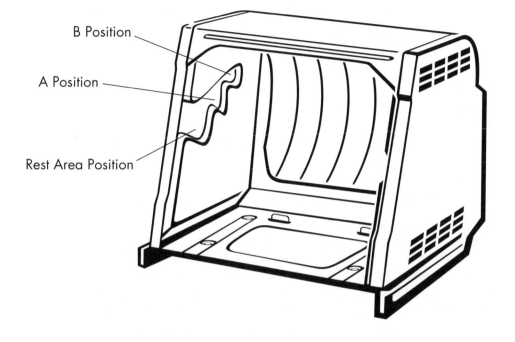

B Position

A Position

Rest Area Position

Know Your Oven

All the recipes in this book have been tested using rotisserie ovens that conform to this basic design. If your oven is different, make the appropriate adjustments or follow manufacturer's instructions.

Some models have a rest area position, which consists of two small grooves on either side of the rotisserie wall, located at the front of the unit. If your model has this feature, this is the place to set the gear wheel assembly when you want to baste meat or vegetables during cooking, arrange hard-to-fit cuts of meat, such as ribs, on the spit rods or position the kabob rods for cooking.

Some rotisserie ovens come with an accessory called a speed basket, which cooks in the B position, closer to the heat source. It is useful as it cooks smaller quantities of food more quickly and browns them more effectively. Most foods are cooked in the A position.

Essential Equipment

In addition to the spit rod/gear wheel assembly and drip tray to catch the melted fat, you will need the following to take full advantage of all the great things your rotisserie oven can cook.

- **A standard rotisserie basket.** The basket is necessary to cook delicate items such as fish and softer vegetables, as well as meat patties and loaves. It can also be used to cook smaller cuts of meat, such as chops.

- **Kabob robs.** These are required for making brochette-type foods, such as souvlaki and skewered vegetables. They are also essential for holding awkward pieces of meat, such as flank steak and ribs, in place on the spit rods.

- **Loading base.** This handy little device holds the gear wheel assembly in place while you load the food onto the spit rods.

- **Rubber-coated heatproof gloves or silicone oven mitts.** The only way to get big pieces of meat, such as whole chickens or roasts, off the spit rods is by using your hands, so you will need gloves that are both washable and heatproof. After you have the food on the platter, you can wash your gloved hands with dishwashing detergent under very hot water, then remove the gloves to let them dry.

- **Instant-read meat thermometer.** It is impossible to be specific about how long food will take to cook since so many factors, such as the amount of bone and fat as well as weight and diameter, influence cooking time. You'll need an instant-read thermometer to ensure that meat is properly cooked.

Desirable Accessories

- **Speed basket.** If your rotisserie oven has a B position, which cooks food closer to the heat source, the speed basket is useful as it cooks smaller quantities of food more quickly and browns them more effectively.

- **Elastic trussing ties.** Although not essential, these ties reduce the time it takes to truss a chicken.

Something to Look For

Check to make sure your basket(s) and drip tray, including cover, have a nonstick surface and are dishwasher-proof. This is a time-saver.

Squeaky Wheel?

As your rotisserie turns, you might hear a dreadful squeak. To avoid this problem, rub the knob on the gear wheel with a bit of vegetable oil before loading it into the oven.

What Can Go Wrong?

The only times you are likely to have problems with your rotisserie are when:

- The food has been incorrectly loaded onto the spit rods. Check your manual for instructions on how to properly balance the item on the rods.
- The food is coming in contact with the heat element and/or the oven. Turn off the oven immediately and fix the problem.

Avoiding Problems

The following steps will help you avoid problems when using your rotisserie oven.

- Make sure the food is properly balanced on the spit rods. Check your manual for the specific loading instructions for your model.
- When using the rotisserie basket, make sure it is securely closed and that no bits of food are protruding beyond the grates. Always add some crumpled-up foil to ensure that raw food fits snugly; it will shrink when cooking and small items may fall out of the basket during rotation.
- Truss whole chickens or turkeys securely. Double-check to make sure that no part of the bird, such as wing tips, extends beyond the circumference of the gear wheels. Trim any excess pieces.
- Before cooking, watch the food rotate for a minute on no-heat rotation to make sure it has been properly set up. If your model doesn't have a no-heat rotation setting, do this with the heat on.

Ingredient Glossary

Asian chili sauce. Made from ground chilies, this spicy Asian condiment is available in many supermarkets as well as Asian markets. It often contains garlic. Sambal oelek is a variety of this sauce. Don't confuse Asian chili sauce with tomato-based chili sauce, which is not spicy and is often substituted for ketchup.

Butter. I always use unsalted butter because I like to season meat with sea salt, which adds texture and flavor.

Garlic. I like to use puréed rather than minced garlic in rubs and coatings because it integrates more fully into the mixture and adheres to food during rotation. Larger particles are likely to fall off as the rotisserie turns. To purée garlic, I use a fine, sharp-toothed grater, such as those made by Microplane®. Minced and sliced garlic or whole cloves can be used in marinades, brines and finishing sauces.

Gingerroot. I like to use puréed rather than minced gingerroot in rubs and coatings for the reasons mentioned above. To purée peeled ginger, use a fine, sharp-toothed grater, such as those made by Microplane®.

Olive oil. I use extra virgin olive oil when making salad dressings or finishing a recipe for its nutrients as well as its taste. However, there's no reason to use extra virgin for cooking because the heat destroys its healthful features. Regular olive oil works just fine for this purpose, so suit yourself.

Sea salt. For rubs and coatings, I use coarse sea salt, which I lightly crush in a mortar. A light crushing maintains the crunchy texture, which I like, but makes the granules small enough to adhere to the meat during rotation. When adding sea salt to cooked food, I prefer a finer texture, coarsely ground. Sometimes I use a salt grinder; other times I use the Rolls Royce of sea salt — fleur de sel — an all-natural sea salt farmed from salt marshes in Brittany, France.

If you can't find coarse sea salt, you can order it online. C Restaurant in Vancouver sells an extensive line of flavored natural sea salts. Visit the store at www.crestaurant.com. Vanns Spices at www.vannsspices.com also has a good selection of plain salts. Most supermarkets sell fine sea salt, which, in my opinion, is preferable to table salt. The quantities can be substituted equally. If you are substituting fine sea salt for coarse, use about one-quarter of the quantity. You'll get the pleasant flavor but not the crunchy texture.

Poultry

IT'S NO SURPRISE THAT ROTISSERIE CHICKENS are one of North America's most popular take-out foods. These succulent birds are readily available and provide an appetizing main course that almost everyone can appreciate. But as tasty as they may be, it's easy to grow tired of prepared rotisserie chickens. In my opinion, they often suffer from a heavy hand with the same old spices and/or an overabundance of barbecue sauce, both of which quickly induce taste bud fatigue. Enter the rotisserie oven. With one of these handy appliances, you can make your own rotisserie chicken with little more effort than it takes to pick one up at the supermarket.

Although few things are easier to prepare than chicken roasted on the rotisserie, the results are sensational. Complemented by just the simplest of seasonings, it bastes in its own juices while the extraneous fat drips off. In roughly an hour (or less if you're cooking cut-up parts), you can produce succulent chicken that's better than Grandma's.

The other reason for roasting chicken in a rotisserie oven is convenience. Once you've made sure the meat is evenly balanced on the spit or kabob rods and isn't coming in contact with any part of the oven, especially the heating element, you can pretty much set the timer and go about your business. If you are roasting a whole chicken, there's one preliminary step. Before loading it onto the spit rods, you'll need to securely truss the bird, a simple procedure that ensures there are no dangling parts to interfere with the smoothly operating rotisserie.

Turkey, duck and game hens respond equally well to rotisserie cooking but, in my opinion, benefit from the additional step of brining. Turkey is drier than chicken, and duck and game hens tend to be chewier, so these meats respond well to a preliminary brining, which increases their moisture content and enhances juiciness. If you're roasting a turkey on the rotisserie (and by all means do — the results are delicious), be aware that you'll need to truss it more securely than a chicken to guarantee that no parts of the bird will come in contact with the oven as it roasts. In my experience, a 10-pound (5 kg) turkey is the maximum even the largest rotisserie oven will accommodate.

TIME AND TEMPERATURE CHART FOR POULTRY

Chicken (whole) or duck	180°F (82°C) 15 minutes/lb (33 minutes/kg)
Chicken pieces (about 3 lbs/1.5 kg total)	
Legs	180°F (82°C)
Breasts	175°F (80°C) 45 minutes total
Ground chicken or turkey (1 lb/500 g)	175°F (80°C) 25 minutes total
Chicken kabobs (2 lbs/1 kg, cut into 1-inch/2.5 cm cubes)	180°F (82°C) 30 to 35 minutes total
Cornish hens (2 cooked side by side)	180°F (82°C) 15 minutes/lb (33 minutes/kg)
Turkey (whole)	180°F (82°C) 15 minutes/lb (33 minutes/kg)

Chicken wings

Thread wings onto the kabob rods, about 3 to a rod, skewering through both halves of each wing and spreading them out as much as possible. Not only does this allow the rods enough space to turn, but it also maximizes the area of skin that is exposed to the heat, producing a browner, crispier result. Wings can also be cooked in the rotisserie basket, if you prefer.

Two small whole chickens

Before loading whole chickens onto the spit rods, securely truss the birds, a simple procedure that ensures there are no dangling parts to interfere with the smooth operation of the rotisserie. After trussing chickens, load them onto the spit rods horizontally through their centers, ensuring they are evenly balanced with a little space between them (as shown in the diagram on the left).

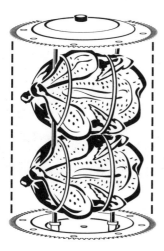

CORRECT

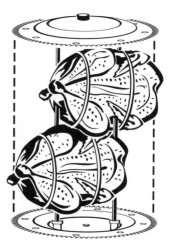

INCORRECT

Chicken legs

Load bone-in chicken legs onto the spit rods so they are evenly balanced, leaving space between them for the heat to circulate, if possible, to ensure even browning. Check to make sure they are not protruding beyond the gear wheels. Legs can also be cooked in the rotisserie basket, if you prefer.

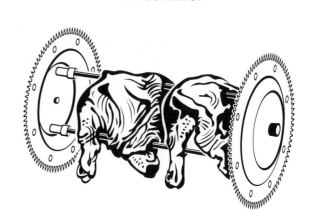

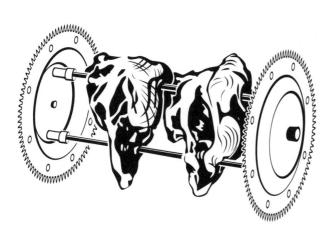

Chicken breasts

Load chicken breasts onto the spit rods horizontally, ensuring they are evenly balanced and leaving enough space between the pieces to allow the heat to circulate. Check to make sure they are not protruding beyond the gear wheels. Breasts can also be cooked in the rotisserie basket, if you prefer.

Turkey

Truss the turkey securely in 4 places, snipping the trussing twine closely at the knot. Load onto the spit rods, ensuring it is evenly balanced. Make sure that no part of the bird comes in contact with the oven as it roasts and that no part of the bird is hanging over the gear wheels, like the piece of leg in the illustration below. If the turkey is not properly positioned, take it off and reload it onto the spit rods.

INCORRECT

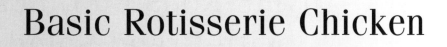

Basic Rotisserie Chicken

SERVES 4 TO 6

Here are the basic instructions for cooking a rotisserie chicken at home. You can customize the seasonings to suit your taste and add variety to stimulate your palate.

Tips

The following basic seasoning blends, which you're likely to have on hand, can be used to prepare a delicious, no-fuss rotisserie chicken:

- salt or seasoned salt and freshly ground black pepper
- lemon pepper
- herbes de Provence
- dried Italian seasoning
- Cajun seasoning
- chili powder
- your favorite spice blend

Trussing a Chicken

To truss a chicken, cut a long piece of butcher's twine, about 3 feet (91 cm). Position it so the midpoint is over the legs and tie them together, winding the twine around each leg, around the thighs and under the wings, then winding it around both wings. Tie tightly at the neck and snip any excess.

1	roasting chicken, 4 to 6 lbs (2 to 3 kg)	1
	Seasoning blend (see Tips, left)	
1 tbsp	olive oil	15 mL

1. Rinse chicken inside and out under cold running water and pat dry with paper towel.

2. Season to taste inside and out with your favorite seasoning blend. Brush with olive oil. Truss chicken securely and load it onto the spit rods, ensuring it is evenly balanced. Roast until an instant-read thermometer inserted into the thickest part of the thigh registers 180°F (82°C), 1 to 1½ hours. Remove from spit rods and transfer to a warm platter. Let rest for 5 minutes before carving.

Variation

Barbecue Chicken: If you're hankering for the flavor of down-home barbecue, simply season the chicken lightly with a complementary seasoning blend, truss and roast as instructed. About 15 minutes before the roasting is finished, turn off the oven and transfer the spit rod assembly, with chicken, to the rest area position if your model has this feature, or follow manufacturer's instructions for glazing. Brush the bird all over with your favorite barbecue sauce, return to the oven, reset the timer and continue roasting until the appropriate temperature is reached.

Thyme-Roasted Chicken with Bread Salad

SERVES 4 TO 6

Here's a special-occasion chicken that is so delicious all your guests will want seconds. The bread salad, an idea I adapted from Judy Rodgers' delightful Zuni Café Cookbook, *is a great way to have "stuffing" with a succulent rotisserie bird.*

Tip

To toast pine nuts: Place nuts in a dry skillet over medium heat and cook, stirring, until they begin to brown, 3 to 4 minutes. Immediately remove from heat and transfer to a small bowl.

Rimmed baking sheet

1	roasting chicken, 4 to 6 lbs (2 to 3 kg)	1
2 tbsp	butter, at room temperature	25 mL
1 tbsp	fresh thyme leaves or 2 tsp (10 mL) dried thyme leaves	15 mL
4	cloves garlic, minced	4
1/2 tsp	grated lemon zest	2 mL
2 tsp	freshly squeezed lemon juice	10 mL

Bread Salad

4 cups	cubed (1-inch/2.5 cm) country-style bread (not sourdough)	1 L
1/2 cup	extra virgin olive oil, divided	125 mL
3	cloves garlic, cut into slivers	3
6	green onions, white part only, cut into 1-inch (2.5 cm) strips	6
2 tbsp	white wine vinegar	25 mL
	Salt and freshly ground black pepper	
2 tbsp	dry white wine	25 mL
1/2 cup	chicken stock	125 mL
2 cups	mixed salad greens	500 mL
2 tbsp	pine nuts, toasted (see Tip, left)	25 mL

1. Rinse chicken inside and out under cold running water and pat dry with paper towel.

2. In a small bowl, cream butter until smooth. Add thyme, garlic, lemon zest and juice, blending until ingredients are well incorporated. Using your fingers or a long blunt utensil such as a chopstick, loosen the skin on the breast and thighs of the chicken. Spread the thyme mixture under the skin as far as you can reach, working it into the meat without breaking the skin. Truss chicken securely and load it onto the spit rods, ensuring it is evenly balanced. Roast until an instant-read thermometer inserted into the thickest part of the thigh registers 180°F (82°C), 1 to 1 1/2 hours.

3. *Bread Salad:* Meanwhile, preheat broiler. In a large bowl, combine bread and 2 tbsp (25 mL) olive oil. Toss to ensure bread is evenly coated. Spread on a rimmed baking sheet and place under preheated broiler, stirring frequently, until nicely browned, about 5 minutes. Transfer to a large serving bowl.

4. In a small skillet, heat 1 tbsp (15 mL) olive oil over medium heat. Add garlic and green onions and cook, stirring, until they begin to brown, about 4 minutes. Add to reserved bread and stir to combine.

5. In a small bowl, combine vinegar and salt and pepper, to taste, stirring well until salt dissolves. Gradually whisk in the remaining olive oil until blended. Add to the bread mixture and toss to combine.

6. Remove chicken from spit rods and transfer to a warm platter. Let rest while you complete the recipe.

7. Meanwhile, pour the liquid from the drip tray into a large measuring cup and let the fat rise to the surface. Spoon off the fat and pour the pan juices, plus any juices from the resting chicken that have collected on the platter, into a small saucepan. Add white wine and chicken stock and bring to a boil over medium heat. Cook until reduced by one-third, about 5 minutes. Sprinkle with salt and freshly ground pepper, to taste. Spoon out 1/4 cup (50 mL) of the mixture, add to the bread cubes and toss well. Spoon the remainder over the carved chicken.

8. Add salad greens and toasted pine nuts to the bread mixture and toss well. Serve the Bread Salad alongside the carved chicken.

Variation

You can make this recipe using 2 smaller chickens, each about 3 1/2 lbs (1.75 kg), roasted side by side on the spit rods (see diagram, page 15). Adjust the roasting time accordingly, until an instant-read thermometer inserted into the thickest part of the thigh registers 180°F (82°C), about 1 hour and 15 minutes.

Herb-Roasted Chicken

SERVES 4 TO 6

This is my favorite recipe for a simple roast chicken. Accompanied by a steaming bowl of creamed spinach and Pot-Roasted New Potatoes (see recipe, page 103) tossed with fresh chives, it makes a fabulous Sunday dinner.

Tip

I like to sprinkle chicken with coarsely ground sea salt or fleur de sel after it's cooked, not only because I like the texture but also because it draws the juices to the surface, increasing succulence.

1	roasting chicken, 4 to 6 lbs (2 to 3 kg)	1
1/4 cup	finely chopped Italian parsley	50 mL
1 tbsp	puréed garlic (see Tip, page 21)	15 mL
1 tsp	grated lemon zest	5 mL
1/2 tsp	freshly ground black pepper	2 mL
1/2 tsp	paprika	2 mL
	Coarsely ground sea salt, optional (see Tip, left)	

1. Rinse chicken inside and out under cold running water and pat dry with paper towel.

2. In a small bowl, combine parsley, garlic, lemon zest and pepper.

3. Using your fingers or a long blunt utensil such as a chopstick, loosen the skin on the breast and thighs of the chicken. Spread the herb mixture under the skin as far as you can reach, working it into the meat without breaking the skin. Sprinkle paprika over chicken. Truss chicken securely and load it onto the spit rods, ensuring it is evenly balanced. Roast until an instant-read thermometer inserted into the thickest part of the thigh registers 180°F (82°C), 1 to 1 1/2 hours.

4. Remove chicken from spit rods and transfer to a warm platter. Sprinkle with sea salt, to taste, if using. Let rest for 5 minutes before carving.

Variations

Olive-Roasted Chicken: For the herb mixture, substitute 1/2 cup (125 mL) pitted black olives, 1/4 cup (50 mL) finely chopped parsley, 2 sun-dried tomatoes in olive oil, minced, 2 cloves garlic, minced, and 1 tsp (5 mL) each grated lemon zest and olive oil. Mix well or process in a mini-chopper until blended. Continue with Step 3.

You can make this recipe using 2 smaller chickens, each about 3 1/2 lbs (1.75 kg), roasted side by side on the spit rods (see diagram, page 15). Adjust the roasting time accordingly, until an instant-read thermometer inserted into the thickest part of the thigh registers 180°F (82°C), about 1 hour and 15 minutes.

French Bistro Chicken

SERVES 4 TO 6

This simple roast chicken, seasoned with rosemary, garlic and lemon, is classic French bistro fare for a reason: it's delicious comfort food. Serve with fluffy garlic mashed potatoes, crisp asparagus and a robust red wine for a great family dinner or an informal meal with friends.

Tip

I like to use puréed garlic in this recipe because it can be evenly distributed under the skin. To purée garlic, use a fine, sharp-toothed grater, such as those made by Microplane®, or put the garlic through a garlic press.

1	roasting chicken, 4 to 6 lbs (2 to 3 kg)	1
1	lemon wedge	1
	Salt and freshly ground black pepper	
	Rosemary sprig	
1 tbsp	minced rosemary leaves	15 mL
1 tbsp	puréed garlic, 3 to 4 cloves (see Tip, left)	15 mL
½ tsp	grated lemon zest	2 mL
1 tbsp	extra virgin olive oil	15 mL
	Coarsely ground sea salt (see Tip, page 20) and freshly ground black pepper	

1. Rinse chicken inside and out under cold running water and pat dry with paper towel. Rub the cavity with the lemon wedge and sprinkle it with salt and pepper, to taste. Place the rosemary sprig and lemon wedge in the cavity.

2. In a small bowl, combine minced rosemary, garlic, lemon zest and olive oil. Using your fingers or a long blunt utensil such as a chopstick, loosen the skin on the breast and thighs of the chicken. Spread the rosemary mixture under the skin, working it into the meat without breaking the skin. Truss chicken securely and load it onto the spit rods, ensuring it is evenly balanced. Roast until an instant-read thermometer inserted into the thickest part of the thigh registers 180°F (82°C), 1 to 1½ hours.

3. Remove chicken from spit rods and transfer to a warm platter. Sprinkle with sea salt and pepper, to taste. Let rest for 5 minutes before carving.

> **Variation**
>
> You can make this recipe using 2 smaller chickens, each about 3½ lbs (1.75 kg), roasted side by side on the spit rods (see diagram, page 15). Adjust the roasting time accordingly, until an instant-read thermometer inserted into the thickest part of the thigh registers 180°F (82°C), about 1 hour and 15 minutes.

Chicken Dukkah

SERVES 4 TO 6

MAKES ABOUT 2 CUPS (500 ML) DUKKAH

Dukkah, an Egyptian blend of nuts seasoned with spices, is usually served as an appetizer with pita bread dipped in olive oil. Perhaps not surprisingly, it also makes a delicious seasoning for roast chicken. Serve this with couscous to continue the Middle Eastern theme.

Prepared dukkah is available in specialty food stores. If you can't find it, you can make your own. I particularly like Ian Hemphill's recipe from **The Spice and Herb Bible.** *It makes a large quantity of dukkah. You can halve the recipe, if you prefer, or make the entire quantity and serve dukkah-dipped pita bread as an appetizer. Cut each pita bread into eight triangles. Provide each of your guests with two little bowls, one containing extra virgin olive oil and the other dukkah. Dip the pita bread into the oil, then the dukkah for a deliciously different treat.*

1	roasting chicken, 4 to 6 lbs (2 to 3 kg)	1
1	lemon wedge	1
	Salt	
2 tbsp	dukkah	25 mL
1 tbsp	olive oil	15 mL
	Coarsely ground sea salt and freshly ground black pepper	

Ian Hemphill's Dukkah

1/4 cup	hazelnuts	50 mL
1/4 cup	pistachio nuts	50 mL
2/3 cup	white sesame seeds	150 mL
1/3 cup	ground coriander seeds (see Tips, right)	75 mL
2 1/2 tbsp	ground cumin seeds	35 mL
1 tsp	salt or to taste	5 mL
1/2 tsp	freshly ground black pepper	2 mL

1. Rinse chicken inside and out under cold running water and pat dry with paper towel. Rub the cavity with the lemon wedge and sprinkle it with salt. Place the lemon wedge in the cavity.

2. *Dukkah:* Roast hazelnuts and pistachio nuts on separate baking sheets in a 350°F (180°C) oven for 15 minutes, until they are fragrant. When the hazelnuts are toasted, place them in a kitchen towel on a cutting board and rub to remove the skins. Coarsely chop nuts in a food processor.

Tips

I prefer the clean, crisp taste and enhanced mineral content of sea salt over refined table salt, which has a bitter, acrid taste. I always have plenty of sea salt on hand in my kitchen, but you can use tiny quantities of table salt in its place, if you prefer.

If you like the taste of coriander and cumin, you can enhance their flavor by toasting the whole seeds before using in the dukkah recipe. Use $\frac{1}{2}$ cup (125 mL) coriander seeds and $\frac{1}{4}$ cup (50 mL) cumin seeds for this quantity of dukkah. Heat them in a dry skillet over medium heat, stirring, until they release their aroma and begin to brown, 3 to 4 minutes. Immediately transfer to a spice grinder or a mortar and grind.

3. Toast sesame seeds in a dry skillet over medium heat, stirring constantly, just until they begin to brown, 3 to 4 minutes. Immediately remove from heat and transfer to a small bowl. Combine with coriander and cumin seeds, hazelnuts, pistachio nuts, and salt and pepper. Refrigerate in an airtight container for up to 3 months.

4. In a small bowl, combine dukkah and olive oil. Using your fingers or a long blunt utensil such as a chopstick, loosen the skin on the breast and thighs of the chicken. Spread the spice mixture under the skin as far as you can reach, working it into the meat without breaking the skin. Truss chicken securely and load it onto the spit rods, ensuring it is evenly balanced. Roast until an instant-read thermometer inserted into the thickest part of the thigh registers 180°F (82°C), 1 to $1\frac{1}{2}$ hours.

5. Remove chicken from spit rods and transfer to a warm platter. Season with salt and pepper, to taste. Let rest for 5 minutes before carving.

Variation

You can make this recipe using 2 smaller chickens, each about $3\frac{1}{2}$ lbs (1.75 kg), roasted side by side on the spit rods (see diagram, page 15). Adjust the roasting time accordingly, until an instant-read thermometer inserted into the thickest part of the thigh registers 180°F (82°C), about 1 hour and 15 minutes.

Chili-Roasted Chicken

SERVES 4 TO 6

If you're looking for a great-tasting chicken that packs a little punch, try this Mexican-style recipe, which uses a chili paste under the skin. I like to serve this with guacamole for an appetizer, and accompany the chicken with refried beans on the side.

Tips

Use New Mexico or guajillo chilies instead of the ancho, if you prefer.

Be sure the chilies are well soaked so they will purée to a smooth paste in the chopper.

I often sprinkle roast chicken and other meats with sea salt or fleur de sel, its more expensive derivation, to enhance the flavor and add texture to the finished result. I don't use refined table salt or kosher salt, which is also refined. In my opinion, table salt has an unpleasant acrid taste and should be used as little as possible in any kitchen.

To crush coarse sea salt: Use a mortar and a pestle, or place the salt between 2 sheets of waxed paper and crush with a rolling pin or the bottom of a measuring cup. The salt should retain its chunky texture but be fine enough to rub evenly over the meat.

2	dried ancho chilies (see Tips, left)	2
1 cup	boiling water	250 mL
2 tbsp	hulled (green) pumpkin seeds	25 mL
1 tbsp	cumin seeds	15 mL
2 tsp	dried oregano leaves	10 mL
2	cloves garlic, chopped	2
1 tbsp	olive oil	15 mL
1	roasting chicken, 4 to 6 lbs (2 to 3 kg)	1
	Coarsely ground sea salt or fleur de sel (see Tips, left) and freshly ground black pepper	

1. In a small bowl, soak chilies in boiling water until soft, 30 minutes. Remove stems, chop chilies coarsely and set aside. Discard soaking liquid.

2. In a dry skillet over medium heat, toast pumpkin and cumin seeds, stirring constantly, until the cumin releases its aroma and the pumpkin seeds pop, watching carefully to ensure the cumin doesn't burn, 3 to 4 minutes. Transfer to a mini-chopper or food processor. Add oregano, garlic, olive oil and reconstituted chilies. Process until smooth.

3. Rinse chicken inside and out under cold running water and pat dry with paper towel. Sprinkle the cavity with salt. Using your fingers or a long blunt utensil such as a chopstick, loosen the skin on the breast and thighs of the chicken. Spread the chili mixture under the skin as far as you can reach, working it into the meat without breaking the skin. Truss chicken securely and load it onto the spit rods, ensuring it is evenly balanced. Roast until an instant-read thermometer inserted into the thickest part of the thigh registers 180°F (82°C), 1 to 1½ hours.

4. Remove chicken from spit rods and transfer to a warm platter. Season with pepper, to taste. Let rest for 5 minutes before carving.

> ## Variation
> You can make this recipe using 2 smaller chickens, each about 3½ lbs (1.75 kg), roasted side by side on the spit rods (see Variation, page 23).

Chicken alla Diavolo

SERVES 4 TO 6

This is an Italian version of chicken with chilies. The chicken is usually marinated in olive oil, lemon juice and crushed dried chilies, but when roasting it on the rotisserie, I've had excellent results using a rub containing lemon zest and cayenne, then dousing the chicken in lemon juice after it's roasted. I like to serve this with a simple risotto (just Arborio rice, onions softened in olive oil and chicken stock) and a sliced tomato salad in season.

Tips

For extra lemon flavor, use lemon-infused oil, available in specialty food shops. Or if you prefer heat, use chili oil.

In this recipe, the salt also helps to balance the acidity of the lemon juice, but if you don't have sea salt on hand, skip this step.

1	roasting chicken, 4 to 6 lbs (2 to 3 kg)	1
1 tbsp	coarse sea salt, crushed (see Tips, page 24)	15 mL
2 tsp	finely grated lemon zest	10 mL
1 tsp	cracked black peppercorns	5 mL
1/4 tsp	cayenne pepper	1 mL
2 tbsp	olive oil, lemon-infused oil or chili oil, divided	25 mL
	Coarsely ground sea salt or fleur de sel, optional (see Tips, page 24)	
1/4 cup	freshly squeezed lemon juice	50 mL

1. Rinse chicken inside and out under cold running water and pat dry with paper towel.

2. In a small bowl, combine sea salt, lemon zest, peppercorns and cayenne. Add just enough oil to make a paste. Using your fingers, work into the skin all over the chicken. Brush chicken with remaining oil and set aside at room temperature for 30 minutes or covered in the refrigerator for 4 hours.

3. Truss chicken securely and load it onto the spit rods, ensuring it is evenly balanced. Roast until an instant-read thermometer inserted into the thickest part of the thigh registers 180°F (82°C), 1 to 1½ hours.

4. Remove chicken from spit rods and transfer to a warm platter. Sprinkle to taste with additional sea salt, if using, and pour lemon juice over top. Let rest for 5 minutes before carving.

Variation

If you prefer, make this recipe using 4 bone-in chicken breasts or legs. Load them onto the spit rods so they are evenly balanced, leaving space between them for the heat to circulate, if possible, to ensure even browning (see diagram, page 16). Reduce roasting time to about 45 minutes, until an instant-read thermometer inserted into the thickest part of the meat registers 175°F (80°C) for breasts and 180°F (82°C) for legs.

Zesty Peach and Pepper Glazed Chicken

SERVES 4

This chicken is so loaded with tasty and intriguing flavors that it's hard to believe it's so easy to make.

Tips

If the peaches in your peach preserves are chunky, chop them finely before combining with the other ingredients.

Chipotle peppers in adobo sauce are available in the Mexican food section of most supermarkets.

1	roasting chicken, about 4 lbs (2 kg)	1
1 tbsp	chili powder	15 mL
1 tbsp	olive oil or chili-infused oil	15 mL
½ cup	peach preserves (see Tips, left)	125 mL
1 tbsp	balsamic vinegar	15 mL
2	chipotle peppers in adobo sauce, finely chopped (see Tips, left)	2

1. Rinse chicken inside and out under cold running water and pat dry with paper towel. Rub skin with chili powder, then brush with oil. Truss chicken securely and load it onto the spit rods, ensuring it is evenly balanced. Roast for 45 minutes.

2. Meanwhile, in a small saucepan over medium heat, combine peach preserves, balsamic vinegar and chipotle peppers. Heat, stirring constantly, until the preserves are melted and the mixture is blended, about 1 minute.

3. When the chicken has roasted for 45 minutes, turn off the oven and transfer the spit rod assembly to the rest area position if your model has this feature, or follow the manufacturer's instructions for glazing. Brush the bird all over with the peach mixture. Return to oven, reset the timer and continue roasting until an instant-read thermometer inserted into the thickest part of the thigh registers 180°F (82°C), about 15 minutes longer.

4. Remove chicken from spit rods and transfer to a warm platter. Cover loosely with foil and let rest for 5 minutes before carving.

Variation

If you prefer, make this recipe using 4 bone-in chicken breasts or legs. Load them onto the spit rods so they are evenly balanced, leaving space between them for the heat to circulate, if possible, to ensure even browning (see diagrams, pages 15 or 16). Brush chicken with the glaze after it has cooked for 30 minutes, then roast for about 15 minutes longer, until an instant-read thermometer inserted into the thickest part of the meat registers 175°F (80°C) for breasts and 180°F (82°C) for legs.

Tandoori Chicken

SERVES 4

Although tandoori actually refers to a kind of clay oven, which cooks chicken at a very high heat, you can approximate the tandoori flavor in a rotisserie oven by using a marinade containing Indian spices. For this recipe, I have used four bone-in chicken breasts or legs, instead of a whole roasting chicken, as the flavor better penetrates the meat if the skin is removed. They fit quite comfortably onto the spit rods if you spear them on the horizontal (see diagrams, pages 15 or 16).

Tip

To toast cumin and coriander seeds: Heat the seeds in a dry skillet over medium heat, stirring frequently, until the spices release their aroma and just begin to brown, 3 to 4 minutes. Immediately transfer to a spice grinder or a mortar and grind. You can also grind the spices on a cutting board using the bottom of a wine bottle or measuring cup.

2 tsp	cumin seeds, toasted and ground (see Tip, left)	10 mL
1 tsp	coriander seeds, toasted and ground	5 mL
3/4 cup	plain yogurt	175 mL
2 tbsp	puréed garlic, 6 to 8 cloves (see Tips, page 32)	25 mL
1 tbsp	puréed gingerroot	15 mL
1 tsp	turmeric	5 mL
1/2 tsp	salt	2 mL
1/2 tsp	cracked black peppercorns	2 mL
1/4 tsp	cayenne pepper	1 mL
4	bone-in chicken breasts or legs, skin removed	4
2 tsp	paprika	10 mL
2 tbsp	finely chopped cilantro, optional	25 mL

1. In a bowl, combine cumin, coriander, yogurt, garlic, gingerroot, turmeric, salt, peppercorns and cayenne. Using a sharp knife, slash the chicken in several places and place in a resealable plastic bag. Add the marinade and toss until chicken is thoroughly coated. Refrigerate for at least 4 hours or preferably overnight.

2. Remove chicken from marinade and pat dry with paper towel. Discard marinade. Sprinkle with paprika. Load chicken onto the spit rods horizontally, leaving space between the pieces to allow the heat to circulate (see diagrams, pages 15 or 16). Roast until an instant-read thermometer inserted into the thickest part of the meat registers 175°F (80°C) for breasts and 180°F (82°C) for legs.

3. Remove chicken from spit rods and transfer to a warm platter. Sprinkle with cilantro, if using, and serve.

Berbere-Spiced Chicken

SERVES 4

Berbere is a spice blend from Ethiopia. It's a lovely combination of hot and sweet, with earthy notes that result from the inclusion of cumin and fenugreek. I like it with chicken, but it also makes a very good rub for swordfish or halibut.

Tips

If you are a heat lover, brush the chicken with chili-infused oil rather than olive oil.

This recipe makes enough berbere for 2 recipes. Store the remainder in an airtight container for up to 1 month.

You can also roast a whole chicken seasoned with berbere. Follow the instructions at right and use about 3 tbsp (45 mL) of the spice blend. Roast the chicken until an instant-read thermometer inserted into the thickest part of the thigh registers 180°F (82°F).

Spice Blend

1 tbsp	cumin seeds	15 mL
1 tbsp	coriander seeds	15 mL
1 tsp	whole black peppercorns	5 mL
1 tsp	whole allspice	5 mL
1 tsp	fenugreek seeds	5 mL
1 tbsp	coarse sea salt, crushed (see Tips, page 24), or 1 tsp (5 mL) table or kosher salt	15 mL
1 tsp	cayenne pepper	5 mL
1 tsp	ground ginger	5 mL
½ tsp	ground cloves	2 mL
½ tsp	ground cinnamon	2 mL
4	bone-in chicken breasts or legs, skin on	4
2 tbsp	olive oil (see Tips, left) Coarsely ground sea salt or fleur de sel, optional Freshly squeezed lemon juice	25 mL

1. *Spice Blend:* In a skillet over medium heat, toast cumin and coriander seeds, black peppercorns, allspice and fenugreek seeds, stirring constantly, until the cumin just begins to brown and releases its aroma, 3 to 4 minutes. Immediately transfer to a mortar or a spice grinder and grind to a fine powder. Add sea salt, cayenne, ginger, cloves and cinnamon and mix well.

2. Sprinkle each chicken piece with 1 tsp (5 mL) of the spice mixture per side, then rub it into the skin. Brush with olive oil. Let stand at room temperature for 30 minutes.

3. Load chicken onto the spit rods horizontally, leaving space between the pieces to allow the heat to circulate (see diagrams, pages 15 or 16). Roast until an instant-read thermometer inserted into the thickest part of the meat registers 175°F (80°C) for breasts and 180°F (82°C) for legs, about 45 minutes.

4. Remove chicken from the spit rods and place on a warm platter. Sprinkle with additional sea salt, if using, and drizzle with lemon juice. Let rest for 5 minutes and serve.

Lemon Cumin Chicken

SERVES 4

The Middle Eastern blend of cumin and lemon is one of my favorite flavor combinations. It's as delicious on chicken as it is in hummus, the traditional chickpea dip. I like to serve this with couscous to continue the regional theme.

Tip

You can use flavored olive oil instead of plain in this recipe. If you prefer more lemon flavor, brush the chicken with lemon-infused oil before cooking. If heat appeals to you, use chili-infused oil instead.

1 tbsp	cumin seeds	15 mL
1 tsp	whole black peppercorns	5 mL
2 tsp	paprika	10 mL
¼ tsp	cayenne pepper	1 mL
1 tbsp	olive oil (see Tip, left)	15 mL
2 tsp	finely grated lemon zest	10 mL
1	lemon	1
1	roasting chicken, about 4 lbs (2 kg)	1
	Coarsely ground sea salt or fleur de sel, optional	

1. In a dry skillet over medium heat, toast cumin seeds and peppercorns until the cumin releases its aroma and just begins to brown, 3 to 4 minutes. Immediately transfer to a spice grinder or a mortar and grind to a fine powder. Add paprika and cayenne and mix well. Transfer to a small bowl and add olive oil and lemon zest. Stir to combine.

2. Cut 4 lengthwise slashes in the lemon and set aside.

3. Rinse the chicken inside and out under cold running water and pat dry with paper towel. Rub the spice blend into the skin of the chicken and sprinkle any excess into the cavity. Stuff the lemon into the cavity. Truss chicken securely and load it onto the spit rods, ensuring it is evenly balanced. Roast until an instant-read thermometer inserted into the thickest part of the thigh registers 180°F (82°C), about 1 hour. Sprinkle with sea salt, if using. Let rest for 5 minutes before carving.

Variation

You can also use this spice blend when roasting 4 bone-in chicken breasts or legs side by side on the spit rods. Omit the whole lemon and roast for about 45 minutes, until an instant-read thermometer inserted into the thickest part of the meat registers 175°F (80°C) for breasts and 180°F (82°C) for legs. Drizzle with 2 tbsp (25 mL) freshly squeezed lemon juice and sprinkle with sea salt, if using, before serving.

Orange Chili Chicken

SERVES 4

The juice of bitter oranges is often used as a flavoring for meats in Mexico. Here, I've added raspberry vinegar to sweet orange juice to produce a similar result. The red currant glaze is the finishing touch.

Tip

To purée garlic: Use a fine, sharp-toothed grater, such as those made by Microplane®, or put the garlic through a garlic press.

2 tsp	finely grated orange zest	10 mL
1 cup	freshly squeezed orange juice	250 mL
2 tbsp	raspberry red wine vinegar	25 mL
2 tsp	puréed garlic, about 2 cloves	10 mL
1	jalapeño pepper, minced	1
½ tsp	cracked black peppercorns	2 mL
4	bone-in chicken breasts or legs, skin on	4

Red Currant Glaze, optional

½ cup	red currant jelly	125 mL
1 tbsp	raspberry red wine vinegar	15 mL
½ tsp	cracked black peppercorns	2 mL

1. In a resealable plastic bag or a shallow dish large enough to accommodate the chicken in a single layer, combine orange zest and juice, vinegar, garlic, jalapeño and peppercorns. Mix well. Add chicken and shake or turn to coat thoroughly with the marinade. Cover and refrigerate for at least 4 hours or overnight.

2. Remove chicken from the marinade. Discard marinade. Load chicken onto the spit rods horizontally, leaving space between the pieces to allow the heat to circulate (see diagrams, pages 15 or 16). Roast for 30 minutes.

3. *Red Currant Glaze:* In a small saucepan over medium heat, combine red currant jelly, vinegar and peppercorns and heat until jelly dissolves. Pour half the mixture into a small dish and set aside. After the chicken has roasted for 30 minutes, turn off the oven and brush the skin with the remainder of the red currant mixture. Reset the timer and roast until an instant-read thermometer inserted into the thickest part of the meat registers 175°F (80°C) for breasts and 180°F (82°C) for legs, about 15 minutes longer.

4. Remove chicken from the spit rods and place on a warm platter. Drizzle with reserved Red Currant Glaze, if using, and serve.

Jamaican-Style Chicken

SERVES 4

If you like Jamaican jerk seasoning, here's a recipe that gives you lots of its flavor but is not as complicated to make as authentic jerk marinade. I like to serve this with coleslaw spiked with pineapple bits.

Tips

To ensure the flavor of the marinade permeates the chicken, gently lift the skin with a blunt object such as a chopstick, without totally detaching it from the meat, before immersing in the marinade.

Try to find Scotch bonnet peppers for this recipe as their unique, slightly smoky flavor captures the island spirit of this dish. If your skin is sensitive, be sure to wear rubber gloves when handling peppers this hot — Scotch bonnet and habanero are among the hottest peppers in the world.

1 tsp	grated lime zest	5 mL
½ cup	freshly squeezed lime juice	125 mL
¼ cup	finely chopped cilantro, stems included	50 mL
4	cloves garlic, minced	4
2 tbsp	vegetable oil	25 mL
1 tbsp	soy sauce	15 mL
1 tbsp	minced gingerroot	15 mL
2	Scotch bonnet or habanero peppers, minced (see Tips, left)	2
1 tbsp	packed brown sugar	15 mL
1 tsp	fresh thyme leaves or ½ tsp (2 mL) dried thyme leaves	5 mL
1 tsp	ground allspice	5 mL
1 tsp	cracked black peppercorns	5 mL
½ tsp	salt	2 mL
4	bone-in chicken breasts or legs, skin on	4

1. In a resealable plastic bag or a shallow dish large enough to accommodate the chicken in a single layer, combine lime zest and juice, cilantro, garlic, vegetable oil, soy sauce, gingerroot, hot peppers, brown sugar, thyme, allspice, peppercorns and salt. Add chicken and shake or turn to coat thoroughly with the marinade. Cover and refrigerate for at least 4 hours or overnight.

2. Remove chicken from the marinade. Discard marinade. Load chicken onto the spit rods horizontally, leaving space between the pieces to allow the heat to circulate (see diagrams, pages 15 or 16). Roast until an instant-read thermometer inserted into the thickest part of the meat registers 175°F (80°C) for breasts and 180°F (82°C) for legs, about 45 minutes. Serve immediately.

Asian-Glazed Chicken

SERVES 4

Rejuvenate your tired taste buds with this delicious Asian-inspired chicken. The plum sauce glaze works well, but if you really need a change, try finishing it with the Orange Chili Glaze (see Variation below). I like to serve this with Chinese Noodles (see recipe, page 109) and stir-fried bok choy.

Tips

To purée garlic and gingerroot: Use a fine, sharp-toothed grater, such as those made by Microplane®.

To toast sesame seeds: Place seeds in a dry skillet over medium heat and cook, stirring, until they begin to brown, 3 to 4 minutes. Immediately remove from heat and transfer to a small bowl.

1	roasting chicken, about 4 lbs (2 kg)	1
1 tbsp	soy sauce, preferably dark	15 mL
1 tbsp	puréed garlic, 3 to 4 cloves (see Tips, left)	15 mL
1 tbsp	puréed gingerroot	15 mL
½ tsp	freshly ground black pepper	2 mL
1 tbsp	sesame oil	15 mL
¼ cup	Asian plum sauce	50 mL
2 tbsp	toasted sesame seeds, optional (see Tips, left)	25 mL

1. Rinse the chicken inside and out under cold running water and pat dry with paper towel.

2. In a small bowl, combine soy sauce, garlic, gingerroot and pepper. Using your fingers or a long blunt utensil such as a chopstick, loosen the skin on the breast and thighs of the chicken. Spread the soy mixture under the skin as far as you can reach and work it into the meat without breaking the skin. Brush the outside of chicken thoroughly with sesame oil.

3. Truss chicken securely and load it onto the spit rods, ensuring it is evenly balanced. Roast for 45 minutes. Turn off the oven and brush the chicken liberally with plum sauce. Reset the timer and continue roasting until an instant-read thermometer inserted into the thickest part of the chicken registers 180°F (82°C), about 15 minutes longer. Sprinkle with toasted sesame seeds, if using. Let rest for 5 minutes before carving.

Variation

Chicken with Orange Chili Glaze: Substitute the following glaze for the plum sauce. In a small bowl, combine 3 tbsp (45 mL) orange marmalade, 1 tbsp (5 mL) soy sauce and 1 tsp (5 mL) Asian chili-garlic sauce. Season with freshly ground black pepper, to taste. Brush the chicken with this glaze for the final 20 minutes of roasting.

Thyme-Roasted Chicken with
Bread Salad (page 18)

Buffalo Chicken Wings

SERVES 4

What would a major sports event be without a big bowl of this American classic? Traditionally, Buffalo wings are deep-fried. Roasted on the rotisserie, these are mouth-watering, with far less fat than the norm.

Tips

These wings are moderately spicy; if you prefer a five-alarm version, add more hot pepper sauce.

Spread out wings as much as possible on the kabob rods. Not only does this allow the rods enough space to turn, but it also maximizes the area of skin that is exposed to the heat, producing a browner, crispier result.

1 tbsp	paprika	15 mL
1 tsp	puréed garlic	5 mL
½ tsp	cayenne pepper	2 mL
½ tsp	hot pepper sauce, or to taste	2 mL
	Freshly ground black pepper	
¼ cup	vegetable oil or melted butter	50 mL
3 lbs	chicken wings, tips removed and patted dry, about 12 wings	1.5 kg
	Coarsely ground sea salt, optional	

Blue Cheese Sauce

½ cup	mayonnaise	125 mL
2 tsp	freshly squeezed lemon juice	10 mL
1 tsp	minced garlic	5 mL
½ tsp	Worcestershire sauce	2 mL
¼ cup	crumbled blue cheese, about 2 oz (60 g)	50 mL
	Freshly ground black pepper	
	Celery sticks	

1. In a bowl large enough to accommodate the wings, combine paprika, garlic, cayenne pepper, hot pepper sauce and black pepper, to taste. Stir well. Gradually stir in vegetable oil until combined. Add chicken wings and toss until they are well coated.

2. Thread wings onto the kabob rods, about 3 to a rod, skewering through both halves of each wing and spreading them out as much as possible (see diagram, page 15). Load onto the spit rods with the spring ends on the right, or according to the manufacturer's instructions for rotation. Roast for about 45 minutes, until the skin is crisp and browned and the juices run clear when the meat is pierced. Transfer wings to a warm platter. Sprinkle lightly with sea salt, if using.

3. *Blue Cheese Sauce:* Meanwhile, in a food processor, combine mayonnaise, lemon juice, garlic, Worcestershire sauce and blue cheese. Process until smooth. Season with black pepper, to taste. Transfer to a small serving bowl.

4. Serve wings with Blue Cheese Sauce and celery sticks for dipping.

Chicken Souvlaki on Pita
(page 36)

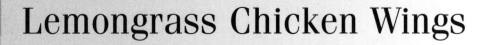

Lemongrass Chicken Wings

SERVES 4

In my opinion, wings are the most luscious part of the chicken. However, because they have more skin in relation to meat than any other part of the bird, they are also high in fat. That's one reason why it's so appealing to roast them on the rotisserie: they lose a substantial amount of fat while retaining the flavor they're famous for. This recipe, which is Thai in origin, is an adaptation of one developed by Andrew Chase, who has a remarkable flair with Asian food.

3	stalks lemongrass, trimmed and chopped	3
¼ cup	freshly squeezed lime juice	50 mL
2 tbsp	fish sauce	25 mL
1 tbsp	minced garlic	15 mL
1 tbsp	minced gingerroot	15 mL
1 tbsp	vegetable oil	15 mL
1 tbsp	granulated sugar	15 mL
2 tsp	Asian chili sauce	10 mL
1 tsp	cracked black peppercorns	5 mL
3 lbs	chicken wings, tips removed, about 12 wings	1.5 kg

Glaze

¼ cup	liquid honey	50 mL
1 to 2	finely chopped fresh Thai chili peppers, optional	1 to 2

1. In a food processor, combine lemongrass, lime juice, fish sauce, garlic, gingerroot, vegetable oil, sugar, chili sauce and peppercorns. Process until smooth. Place chicken wings in a bowl and pour sauce over top. Cover and marinate for 4 hours or preferably overnight.

2. Remove wings from marinade. Discard marinade.

3. *Glaze:* In a bowl, combine honey and chilies, if using. Set aside.

4. Thread wings onto the kabob rods, about 3 to a rod, skewering through both halves of each wing and spreading them out as much as possible (see diagram, page 15). Load onto the spit rods with the spring ends on the right, or according to the manufacturer's instructions for rotation. Roast for 30 minutes. Turn off the oven and brush with glaze. Reset the timer and continue roasting until the skin is crisp and browned and the juices run clear when the meat is pierced, about 15 minutes.

Maple Soy–Glazed Chicken Wings

SERVES 4

You can't go wrong with this simple recipe, which always generates requests for seconds. The cooked marinade makes a great dipping sauce and can be enhanced with the addition of a hot pepper to please heat seekers. Any way you serve it, this is great finger food.

Tips

If you prefer, place the cooked wings in a serving bowl and pour the dipping sauce over them. Toss well to ensure they are evenly coated.

To purée garlic and gingerroot: Use a fine, sharp-toothed grater, such as those made by Microplane®.

¼ cup	soy sauce	50 mL
¼ cup	pure maple syrup	50 mL
2 tbsp	sherry	25 mL
2 tbsp	rice vinegar	25 mL
1 tbsp	puréed garlic, 3 to 4 cloves (see Tips, left)	15 mL
1 tbsp	puréed gingerroot	15 mL
3 lbs	chicken wings, tips removed, about 12 wings	1.5 kg
1	long red or green chili pepper, minced, optional	1

1. In a bowl large enough to accommodate the chicken, combine soy sauce, maple syrup, sherry, rice vinegar, garlic and gingerroot. Add chicken and toss until wings are thoroughly coated. Cover and refrigerate for at least 4 hours or overnight.

2. Remove wings from marinade and reserve marinade. Thread wings onto the kabob rods, about 3 to a rod, skewering through both halves of each wing and spreading them out as much as possible (see diagram, page 15). Load onto the spit rods with the spring ends on the right, or according to the manufacturer's instructions for rotation. Roast until wings are golden brown and crispy and the juices run clear when the meat is pierced, about 40 minutes.

3. Meanwhile, in a small saucepan over medium heat, combine reserved marinade and chili pepper, if using. Bring to a boil. Reduce heat to low and simmer for 10 minutes. Serve alongside wings as a dipping sauce.

Chicken Souvlaki on Pita

SERVES 6 TO 8

Served with a big Greek salad, this makes a delicious weeknight dinner or the perfect dish for a casual evening with friends. If you prefer, you can use store-bought tzatziki for convenience. Save any extra and use as a dip for crudités.

Tips

If you prefer a more intense lemon flavor, add 1 tsp (5 mL) grated lemon zest to the marinade or replace 2 tbsp (25 mL) of the olive oil with lemon-infused oil.

If you can't find Greek-style yogurt, which is very thick, you can make your own. Simply line a strainer with cheesecloth, fill with 3 cups (750 mL) plain full-fat yogurt and let sit in the refrigerator overnight. Discard the accumulated liquid and measure out 1 cup (250 mL) of the thick yogurt. Serve any excess with liquid honey for a tasty treat.

½ cup	olive oil	125 mL
¼ cup	freshly squeezed lemon juice	50 mL
¼ cup	dry white wine	50 mL
1 tbsp	puréed garlic, 3 to 4 cloves (see Tips, page 30)	15 mL
2 tsp	dried oregano leaves	10 mL
1 tsp	cracked black peppercorns	5 mL
1 tsp	coarse sea salt, crushed (see Tips, page 24)	5 mL
2	bay leaves, crumbled	2
2 lbs	skinless boneless chicken, cut into 1½-inch (4 cm) cubes	1 kg

Tzatziki

1 cup	Greek-style yogurt (see Tips, left)	250 mL
1	English cucumber, peeled and shredded	1
1 tbsp	extra virgin olive oil	15 mL
1 tsp	puréed garlic	5 mL
1 tsp	freshly squeezed lemon juice	5 mL
	Warm pita bread	
	Sliced Spanish onion	
	Tomato wedges	
	Shredded lettuce	

1. In a bowl, combine oil, lemon juice, wine, garlic, oregano, peppercorns, salt and bay leaves. Add chicken and toss to coat. Cover and refrigerate for 4 hours or overnight.

2. *Tzatziki:* In a bowl, combine yogurt, cucumber, olive oil, garlic and lemon juice. Cover and refrigerate until flavors are blended, about 2 hours, or for up to a week.

3. Remove chicken from the marinade. Discard marinade. Pat dry with paper towel and thread onto the kabob rods, leaving space between the pieces for the heat to circulate. Load onto the spit rods with the spring ends on the right, or according to manufacturer's instructions for rotation. Roast until chicken is no longer pink inside, 30 to 35 minutes.

4. To serve, spread warm pita bread with tzatziki and arrange 3 or 4 pieces of chicken in the middle of each. Garnish with any combination of onion, tomato and/or lettuce. Fold the bread over to form a roll and enjoy.

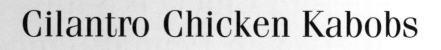

Cilantro Chicken Kabobs

SERVES 6 TO 8

These tasty chicken kabobs are Asian in spirit and pack a rich cilantro flavor. They make a great informal dinner accompanied by fluffy white rice and a simple salad such as sliced cucumbers in an Asian-flavored vinaigrette (see Tips, below).

Tips

Eight sprigs of cilantro yields about 100 cilantro leaves.

To make Asian Cucumber Salad: Whisk together 2 tbsp (25 mL) rice vinegar, 1 tbsp (15 mL) soy sauce and 1 tbsp (15 mL) olive oil in a serving bowl. Peel a cucumber and slice it thinly. Add to vinaigrette and toss to combine. Season with salt and pepper, to taste.

10	sprigs cilantro, leaves and stems, no roots	10
¼ cup	soy sauce	50 mL
1 tbsp	olive oil	15 mL
1 tbsp	rice wine vinegar	15 mL
2 tsp	cracked black peppercorns	10 mL
2 tsp	oyster sauce	10 mL
6	cloves garlic	6
¼ tsp	cayenne pepper	1 mL
2 lbs	skinless boneless chicken, cut into 1-inch (2.5 cm) cubes	1 kg

Dipping Sauce

1 cup	water	250 mL
½ cup	granulated sugar	125 mL
8	sprigs cilantro, leaves only	8
2	cloves garlic	2
3 tbsp	freshly squeezed lime juice	45 mL
1 tbsp	Asian chili sauce	15 mL
1 tbsp	fish sauce	15 mL
½ cup	peanuts, optional	125 mL

1. In a food processor, combine cilantro, soy sauce, olive oil, vinegar, peppercorns, oyster sauce, garlic and cayenne. Process until smooth.

2. In a resealable plastic bag, combine chicken and marinade. Seal and toss until chicken is coated. Refrigerate for 4 hours or overnight.

3. *Dipping Sauce:* In a saucepan, combine water and sugar. Bring to a boil over medium heat and cook until syrupy, about 10 minutes. Let cool. In a food processor, combine cilantro, garlic, lime juice, chili sauce, fish sauce and peanuts, if using. Add cooled syrup and process until smooth.

4. Remove chicken from the marinade. Discard marinade. Pat dry with paper towel and thread onto the kabob rods, leaving space between pieces to allow the heat to circulate. Load onto the spit rods with the spring ends on the right, or according to the manufacturer's instructions for rotation. Roast until the chicken is no longer pink inside, 30 to 35 minutes. Remove from skewers and serve immediately accompanied by Dipping Sauce.

Chicken Satay
with Peanut Sauce

SERVES 6 TO 8

*Satay, a traditional Thai
dish served on tiny wooden
skewers, has become a
fashionable North American
party food. This recipe
moves it to the table, where,
as in Thailand, it is served
as a family meal. Fluffy
white rice and steamed
spinach, sprinkled with
toasted sesame seeds, make
great accompaniments.*

Tips

If you don't have fresh
limes, substitute lemon zest
and juice in the chicken
marinade.

To purée garlic and gingerroot:
Use a fine, sharp-toothed
grater, such as those made
by Microplane®.

¼ cup	soy sauce	50 mL
½ tsp	grated lime zest	2 mL
2 tbsp	freshly squeezed lime juice	25 mL
1 tbsp	fish sauce	15 mL
1 tbsp	vegetable oil	15 mL
1 tsp	granulated sugar	5 mL
1 tsp	grated gingerroot	5 mL
1 tsp	Asian chili sauce	5 mL
1 tsp	puréed garlic	5 mL
2 lbs	skinless boneless chicken, cut into 1-inch (2.5 cm) cubes	1 kg

Peanut Sauce

½ cup	smooth peanut butter	125 mL
¼ cup	warm water	50 mL
1 tbsp	soy sauce	15 mL
1 tbsp	rice vinegar	15 mL
2 tsp	toasted sesame oil	10 mL
2 tsp	puréed gingerroot	10 mL
2 tsp	puréed garlic, about 2 cloves	10 mL
1 tsp	granulated sugar	5 mL
2 tbsp	chopped cilantro, optional	25 mL
1	long red chili pepper, finely chopped, optional	1
1 tbsp	finely chopped roasted peanuts, optional	15 mL

1. In a bowl large enough to accommodate the chicken, combine soy sauce, lime zest and juice, fish sauce, vegetable oil, sugar, gingerroot, chili sauce and garlic. Add chicken to bowl and toss to coat. Set aside to marinate at room temperature for 30 minutes.

2. Remove chicken from the marinade. Discard marinade. Pat dry with paper towel and thread onto the kabob rods, leaving space between the pieces to allow the heat to circulate. Load onto the spit rods with the spring ends on the right, or according to the manufacturer's instructions for rotation. Roast until the chicken is no longer pink inside, 30 to 35 minutes. Remove from skewers and serve with Peanut Sauce.

3. *Peanut Sauce:* Meanwhile, in a blender, combine peanut butter, warm water, soy sauce, vinegar, sesame oil, gingerroot, garlic, sugar and cilantro and/or chili pepper, if using. Blend until mixture is smooth, about 30 seconds. Serve in individual bowls for dipping and garnish with roasted peanuts, if using.

Cornish Hens with Red Currant Glaze

SERVES 2 TO 4

Nothing could be simpler than this tasty dish: crisp roasted game hens finished with a sweet red currant glaze. Although it is not essential, I find that brining the hens for an hour or two before roasting improves both the texture and the flavor of the meat, but if you don't have time, you can skip this step. If you need to serve four people, buy larger hens and cut them in half down the breastbone after they have finished roasting.

Tip

For seasoning salt, use your favorite brand-name blend or a simple combination such as onion or celery salt.

Brine

1/2 cup	kosher salt or 1/4 cup (50 mL) table salt	125 mL
1 tsp	seasoned salt (see Tip, left)	5 mL
2 cups	boiling water	500 mL
6 cups	cold water (approx.) Ice cubes	1.5 L
2	rock Cornish hens, each 1 to 1 1/2 lbs (500 to 750 g)	2
1 tsp	dried thyme leaves, crumbled	5 mL
1/4 tsp	salt	1 mL
1/4 tsp	freshly ground black pepper	1 mL
2 tbsp	olive oil	25 mL

Red Currant Glaze

1/2 cup	red currant jelly	125 mL
1 tbsp	balsamic vinegar	15 mL
1/2 tsp	cracked black peppercorns	2 mL

1. *Brine:* In a non-reactive bowl large enough to easily accommodate the hens and brining liquid, combine kosher salt, seasoned salt and boiling water. Stir well until the salt is dissolved, then add cold water and enough ice cubes to cool the solution to room temperature. Add the hens. Add additional water, if necessary, to cover. Cover and refrigerate for 1 to 2 hours.

2. Remove hens from the brine. Discard brine. Rinse hens well inside and out under cold running water and pat dry with paper towel. In a small bowl, combine thyme, salt and pepper. Rub into the skin of the birds, then brush all over with olive oil. Carefully truss, making sure the legs and wings are secure. Load the hens onto the spit rods side by side, leaving space between them to allow for even browning. Roast for 30 minutes.

3. *Red Currant Glaze:* Meanwhile, in a small saucepan over medium heat, combine red currant jelly, balsamic vinegar and peppercorns. Heat, stirring, until the jelly is dissolved. Pour half the mixture into a small dish and set aside. After the birds have roasted for 30 minutes, turn off the oven and brush the hens all over with the remainder of the Red Currant Glaze. Reset the timer and roast until an instant-read thermometer inserted into the thickest part of the thigh registers 180°F (82°C), about 15 minutes longer.

4. Transfer hens to a warm platter and let rest for 5 minutes. If you are serving 4 people, place 1 hen on a cutting board, cut in half down the breastbone and return to platter, skin side up. Repeat with second hen. Pour reserved Red Currant Glaze over the birds to serve.

Variation

Cornish Hens with Whiskey and Mango Glaze: Substitute a glaze made of mango chutney and whiskey for the red currant one. In a food processor or mini-chopper, combine ¼ cup (50 mL) mango chutney, 2 tbsp (25 mL) bourbon or other blended whiskey, 2 tsp (10 mL) Dijon mustard, 2 tsp (10 mL) soy sauce and 1 tsp (5 mL) minced gingerroot. Pulse several times until chutney is puréed and mixture is blended. Follow the instructions for using the Red Currant Glaze.

Thai-Style Hens in Coconut Curry Sauce

SERVES 2 TO 4

Here's a Thai-inspired dish that is delicious and unusual. Serve this with lots of fluffy white rice to soak up the sauce and, if you're serving wine, consider a chilled Riesling with a hint of sweetness to complement the spice.

Brine

2 tbsp	kosher salt or 1 tbsp (15 mL) table salt	25 mL
1 cup	boiling water	250 mL
2 tsp	Thai red curry paste	10 mL
½ cup	unsweetened coconut milk	125 mL
6 cups	cold water (approx.)	1.5 L
	Ice cubes	
2	rock Cornish hens, each 1 to 1½ lbs (500 to 750 g)	2
1 tbsp	olive oil	15 mL
2 to 3 tbsp	red pepper jelly, slightly warmed	25 to 45 mL

Coconut Curry Sauce

1 cup	unsweetened coconut milk	250 mL
1	stalk lemongrass, smashed and cut into 1-inch (2.5 cm) rounds	1
1 tsp	Thai red curry paste	5 mL
¼ tsp	grated lime zest	1 mL
1 tbsp	freshly squeezed lime juice	15 mL
1 tsp	fish sauce	5 mL
¼ tsp	freshly ground black pepper	1 mL
Pinch	granulated sugar	Pinch
	Finely chopped cilantro, optional	

1. *Brine:* In a non-reactive bowl large enough to easily accommodate the hens and brining liquid, combine kosher salt and boiling water. Stir until the salt is dissolved. Add curry paste, coconut milk, cold water and enough ice cubes to cool the solution to room temperature. Add hens and additional water, if necessary, to cover. Cover bowl and refrigerate for 1 to 2 hours.

2. Remove hens from the brine. Discard brine. Rinse well inside and out under cold running water and pat dry with paper towel. Brush hens all over with olive oil. Carefully truss, making sure the legs and wings are secure. Load the hens onto the spit rods side by side, leaving space between them to allow for even browning. Roast for about 30 minutes. Turn off the oven and baste generously with red pepper jelly. Reset the timer and continue roasting until an instant-read thermometer inserted into the thickest part of the thigh registers 180°F (82°C), about 20 minutes longer.

3. *Coconut Curry Sauce:* Meanwhile, in a saucepan, heat coconut milk and lemongrass over medium heat until almost at the boiling point. (Don't let it boil.) Add curry paste and cook, stirring, for 2 minutes. Reduce heat to low and stir in lime zest and juice, fish sauce, pepper and sugar. Cook, stirring, for 2 minutes. Remove from heat and strain if desired. Keep warm until ready to use.

4. When hens are cooked, transfer to a warm platter and let rest for 5 minutes. If serving 4 people, place 1 hen on a cutting board and cut in half down the breastbone. Return to platter, skin side up. Repeat with second hen. Pour sauce over hens and garnish with cilantro, if using.

Cornish Hens with Tarragon

SERVES 2 TO 4

Tarragon is one of my favorite seasonings for poultry, and this is one of my favorite ways of roasting game hens. You'll be amazed at how much flavor this simple tarragon butter, placed under the skin before roasting, adds to the meat. Brushing the skin with a bit of melted apple or white wine jelly during the last 15 minutes of roasting crisps the skin to a beautiful golden brown. Yum.

Tip

I like to use puréed garlic in this recipe because it can be evenly distributed under the skin. To purée garlic, use a fine, sharp-toothed grater, such as those made by Microplane®, or put the garlic through a garlic press.

Brine

1/2 cup	kosher salt or 1/4 cup (50 mL) table salt	125 mL
2	cloves garlic, coarsely chopped	2
10	whole black peppercorns	10
2 cups	boiling water	500 mL
6 cups	cold water (approx.)	1.5 L
	Ice cubes	
2	rock Cornish hens, each 1 to 1 1/2 lbs (500 to 750 g)	2
2 tbsp	butter, at room temperature	25 mL
1 tbsp	finely chopped tarragon	15 mL
2 tsp	grated lemon zest	10 mL
2 tsp	puréed garlic, about 2 cloves	10 mL
3 tbsp	apple or white wine jelly, melted	45 mL

1. *Brine:* In a non-reactive container large enough to easily accommodate the hens and brining liquid, combine salt, garlic, peppercorns and boiling water. Stir until the salt is dissolved. Add cold water and enough ice cubes to cool the solution to room temperature. Add hens and additional cold water, if necessary, to cover. Cover the bowl and refrigerate for 1 to 2 hours.

2. Remove hens from the brine. Discard brine. Rinse hens well inside and out under cold running water and pat dry with paper towel.

3. In a small bowl or a mini-chopper, combine butter, tarragon, lemon zest and garlic. Starting at the breastbone, gently lift the skin of each hen and spread the butter mixture over the breast and thighs. Carefully truss, making sure the legs and wings are secure. Load the hens onto the spit rods side by side, leaving space between them to allow for even browning. Roast for 30 minutes. Turn off the oven and baste the hens generously with apple jelly. Reset the timer and continue roasting until an instant-read thermometer inserted into the thickest part of the thigh registers 180°F (82°C), about 15 minutes longer.

4. When hens are cooked, transfer to a warm platter and let rest for 5 minutes. If serving 4 people, place 1 hen on a cutting board and cut in half down the breastbone. Return to platter, skin side up. Repeat with second hen.

Chinese-Glazed Duck

SERVES 4

A classic and delicious way to prepare duck. Serve this with vegetable fried rice and stir-fried bok choy to continue the Asian theme.

Tips

Be sure to remove the giblets from the cavity before brining. A stainless steel stockpot works well for brining larger birds such as duck and turkey.

Searing the duck helps produce a crispier skin. If you prefer an even crispier skin, after removing the duck from the brine, rinsing and patting it dry, place it upright in a bowl and refrigerate for about 4 hours. Continue with Step 2.

To purée garlic and gingerroot: Use a fine, sharp-toothed grater, such as those made by Microplane®.

Brine

½ cup	kosher salt or ¼ cup (50 mL) table salt	125 mL
3	cloves garlic, peeled and sliced	3
10	whole black peppercorns	10
1 tbsp	packed brown sugar	15 mL
2 cups	boiling water	500 mL
8 cups	cold water (approx.)	2 L
	Ice cubes	
1	duck, 4 to 5 lbs (2 to 2.5 kg)	1
1 tbsp	puréed garlic, 3 to 4 cloves (see Tips, left)	15 mL
1 tbsp	puréed gingerroot	15 mL
½ tsp	sea salt	2 mL
½ tsp	freshly ground black pepper	2 mL

Hoisin Glaze

3 tbsp	hoisin sauce	45 mL
2 tbsp	orange-flavored liqueur	25 mL
1 tsp	soy sauce	5 mL

1. *Brine:* In a non-reactive container or a bowl large enough to easily accommodate the duck and brining liquid, combine salt, garlic, peppercorns and brown sugar. Add boiling water and stir until the salt dissolves. Add cold water and enough ice cubes to cool the solution to room temperature. Add the duck and additional cold water, if necessary, to cover. Cover the container and refrigerate for at least 6 hours or overnight.

2. Remove duck from brine. Discard brine. Rinse duck thoroughly inside and out under cold running water and pat dry with paper towel. Prick the skin all over with the tines of a fork, being careful not to puncture the meat.

3. In a small bowl, combine garlic, gingerroot, salt and pepper. Rub the mixture into the cavity of the duck. Cut off wing tips and truss duck. Load duck onto the spit rods, ensuring it is evenly balanced. Roast for 45 minutes, then position the duck in front of the heating element and press the "pause to sear" setting for 4 minutes.

4. *Hoisin Glaze:* Meanwhile, in a small bowl, combine hoisin sauce, orange-flavored liqueur and soy sauce.

5. After the duck has roasted and been seared, turn off the oven and baste the duck all over with the glaze. Reset the timer and roast until an instant-read thermometer inserted into the thickest part of the thigh registers 180°F (82°C), about 20 minutes longer.

Roast Turkey with Mushrooms and Tarragon

SERVES 10

I love the flavors of the porcini mushrooms and tarragon in this absolutely delicious preparation for a turkey. Serve this to your family for a holiday feast or delight your most discriminating guests with this unusual combination.

Tips

Turkey tends to dry out during roasting, but brining it helps to keep the meat moist and succulent. I like to use a lightly salted solution for turkey and leave it in the brine overnight. A large stainless steel stockpot works well for this.

To calculate the cooking time for different-size turkeys, use the guideline of about 15 minutes per pound (33 minutes per kg).

When buying a turkey for a rotisserie oven, pay close attention to the size. Ten pounds (5 kg) is the maximum weight my large rotisserie will accommodate.

Brine

1 cup	kosher salt or ½ cup (125 mL) table salt	250 mL
4 cups	boiling water	1 L
6 quarts	cold water (approx.)	6 L
	Ice cubes	
1	turkey, about 10 lbs (5 kg)	1
2	packages (each 1 oz/30 g) dried porcini mushrooms	2
2 cups	boiling water	500 mL
2 tbsp	butter	25 mL
1 tbsp	puréed garlic, 3 to 4 cloves (see Tips, right)	15 mL
2 tbsp	finely chopped fresh tarragon or 2 tsp (10 mL) crumbled dried tarragon	25 mL
1 tsp	grated lemon zest	5 mL

1. In a non-reactive container large enough to easily accommodate the turkey and brining liquid, combine salt and boiling water. Stir well until the salt dissolves. Add cold water and enough ice cubes to cool the solution to room temperature.

2. Remove giblets from the turkey cavity and rinse thoroughly inside and out under cold running water. Add turkey to the brining solution along with additional cold water, if necessary, to cover the bird completely. Cover the container and refrigerate overnight, at least 8 hours, or up to 18 hours.

3. Remove turkey from the brine. Discard brine. Rinse turkey thoroughly under cold running water. Pat dry with paper towel and set aside while preparing the mushrooms.

Although there is no use for the mushroom soaking liquid in this recipe, you can refrigerate it for several days and use it to flavor soups, stews and stocks.

I like to use puréed garlic in this recipe because it can be evenly distributed under the skin. To purée garlic, use a fine, sharp-toothed grater, such as those made by Microplane®, or put the garlic through a garlic press.

4. Meanwhile, in a heatproof bowl, combine mushrooms and boiling water. Soak for 20 minutes. Drain, discarding soaking liquid (see Tips, left). Pat dry with paper towel and chop finely.

5. In a skillet, melt butter over medium heat. Add mushrooms and cook, stirring, for 3 minutes. Add garlic and cook, stirring, for 1 minute. Remove from heat. Stir in tarragon and lemon zest. Let cool until lukewarm.

6. Using a long blunt object such as a chopstick, gently lift up the skin of the turkey over the breast and thighs. Spread the mushroom mixture under the skin as far as you can reach, working it into the meat without breaking the skin.

7. Truss turkey securely in 4 places (see diagram, page 16). Snip trussing twine closely at the knot. Load onto the spit rods, ensuring it is evenly balanced. Roast until an instant-read thermometer inserted into the thickest part of the thigh registers 180°F (82°C), about 2½ hours.

Chili-Roasted Turkey

SERVES 10

*From time to time, I like
to roast a turkey for a
non-holiday meal. Here's a
delicious and untraditional
presentation that has its
roots in Mexican cuisine.
I've served this with great
success at an alfresco dinner
on a warm summer night,
accompanied by a corn
and black bean salad and
roasted Vidalia onions.*

Tips

Ancho, New Mexico and
guajillo chilies are mild to
medium-hot chilies widely
available in dried form. They
can be used interchangeably
in this recipe. Chipotle
peppers in adobo sauce are
medium hot but have quite
a smoky flavor. They come
in cans and are available in
large grocery stores and
specialty food stores.

Achiote seeds, also known
as annatto, are used widely
in Latin American cooking,
mainly as a coloring agent.
They have a slightly bitter
but pleasant flavor when
used with discretion. If you
can't find them, don't be
concerned; the turkey is
delicious with or without
them.

Brine

1 cup	kosher salt or ½ cup (125 mL) table salt	250 mL
4	cloves garlic, sliced	4
10	whole black peppercorns	10
2	dried red chili peppers, crumbled, or 2 tsp (10 mL) hot pepper flakes	2
4 cups	boiling water	1 L
6 quarts	cold water (approx.)	6 L
	Ice cubes	
1	turkey, about 10 lbs (5 kg)	1
4	dried ancho, New Mexico or guajillo chili peppers, (see Tips, left)	4
2 cups	boiling water	500 mL
4	chipotle peppers in adobo sauce	4
¼ cup	butter, at room temperature	50 mL
4	cloves garlic, minced	4
1 tsp	dried oregano leaves	5 mL
½ tsp	salt	2 mL
½ tsp	cracked black peppercorns	2 mL
	Ground achiote seeds, optional (see Tips, left)	
2 tbsp	olive oil	25 mL

1. *Brine:* In a non-reactive container large enough to easily accommodate the turkey and brining liquid, combine salt, garlic, peppercorns, red chilies and boiling water. Stir until the salt dissolves. Add cold water and enough ice cubes to cool the solution to room temperature.

2. Remove giblets from the turkey cavity and rinse thoroughly inside and out under cold running water. Add turkey to brining solution along with additional cold water, if necessary, to cover the bird completely. Cover the container and refrigerate overnight, at least 8 hours, or up to 18 hours.

3. Remove turkey from the brine. Discard brine. Rinse turkey thoroughly under cold running water. Pat dry with paper towel and set aside while preparing the seasoning.

4. In a heatproof bowl, soak dried chilies in boiling water for 30 minutes. Remove stems, chop finely and place in a food processor or mini-chopper. Add chipotle peppers in adobo sauce, butter, garlic, oregano, salt and peppercorns and pulse until smoothly blended.

5. Using a long blunt object such as a chopstick, gently lift the skin of the turkey over the breast and thighs. Spread the chili mixture under the skin as far as you can reach, working into the meat without breaking the skin.

6. Rub the skin of the turkey with achiote, if using. Brush liberally with olive oil.

7. Truss turkey securely in 4 places (see diagram, page 16). Snip trussing twine closely at the knot. Load onto the spit rods, ensuring it is evenly balanced. Roast until an instant-read thermometer inserted into the thickest part of the thigh registers 180°F (82°C), about $2\frac{1}{2}$ hours.

Traditional Turkey Breast with Sage and Onion Stuffing

SERVES 4

If you don't have a large group to cook for, here's a delicious holiday turkey, complete with oven-baked stuffing. Add a bowl of fluffy mashed potatoes and cranberry sauce and you're well on your way to a feast with all the trimmings.

Tips

If you like a crunchy top on stuffing, remove the foil for the final 10 minutes of roasting.

To crush coarse sea salt: Use a mortar and a pestle, or place the salt between 2 sheets of waxed paper and crush with a rolling pin or the bottom of a measuring cup. The salt should retain its chunky texture but be fine enough to rub evenly over the meat.

Brine

1/2 cup	kosher salt or 1/4 cup (50 mL) table salt	125 mL
2	cloves garlic, chopped	2
10	whole black peppercorns	10
2 cups	boiling water	500 mL
8 cups	cold water (approx.)	2 L
	Ice cubes	
1	bone-in turkey breast, skin on, about 3 lbs (1.5 kg)	1
1/2 tsp	dried thyme leaves	2 mL
1/2 tsp	ground dried sage	2 mL
1/2 tsp	coarse sea salt, crushed (see Tips, left), or 1/4 tsp (1 mL) table salt	2 mL
1/2 tsp	cracked black peppercorns	2 mL
1 tbsp	olive oil	15 mL

Stuffing

4 cups	stale bread cubes	1 L
1	onion, finely chopped	1
20	fresh sage leaves, finely chopped, or 1 tsp (5 mL) ground sage	20
3	stalks celery, finely chopped	3
1 tsp	salt	5 mL
1/2 tsp	poultry seasoning	2 mL
1/4 tsp	freshly ground black pepper	1 mL
1/4 cup	melted butter	50 mL

1. *Brine:* In a non-reactive container large enough to easily accommodate the turkey and brining liquid, combine salt, garlic, peppercorns and boiling water. Stir until the salt is dissolved. Add cold water and enough ice cubes to cool the solution to room temperature. Add turkey breast and additional water, if necessary, to cover the breast completely. Cover the container and refrigerate for 3 hours.

2. Remove turkey from the brine. Discard brine. Rinse turkey thoroughly under cold running water and pat dry with paper towel.

3. In a small bowl, combine thyme, sage, salt and peppercorns. Rub into the skin side of the turkey. Brush with olive oil. Load onto the spit rods, ensuring that both sides of the breast are secure and it is evenly balanced. (You can tie the turkey breast with string, if necessary, being sure to clip any dangling ends.) Roast until an instant-read thermometer inserted into the thickest part of the breast registers 170°F (77°C), about 1½ hours.

4. *Stuffing:* Meanwhile, preheat oven to 350°F (180°C). Grease a 4-cup (1 L) baking dish. In a large bowl, combine bread, onion, sage, celery, salt, poultry seasoning and pepper. Using your hands, toss to combine. Pour butter evenly over mixture. Transfer to prepared baking dish. Cover loosely with foil and bake in preheated oven until hot, about 1 hour (see Tips, left).

5. Remove turkey from the spit rods and place on a platter. Let rest for 5 minutes before carving. Serve stuffing alongside.

Variation

Holiday Turkey with Sage and Onion Stuffing: Substitute a whole turkey no larger than 10 lbs (5 kg) for the turkey breast. Triple the quantity of brine, rub and stuffing and refrigerate turkey in brining solution overnight before roasting. Truss and roast according to the instructions in Step 7, page 51. Prepare the stuffing as in Step 4.

Turkey Burgers with Chipotle Mayo

SERVES 4

Served with a simple green salad, here's a great dinner the whole family will enjoy.

Tip

To toast cumin seeds: Place seeds in a dry skillet over medium heat and cook, stirring, until they release their aroma and just begin to brown, 3 to 4 minutes. Immediately transfer to a spice grinder or a mortar and grind.

Chipotle Mayo

½ cup	prepared mayonnaise	125 mL
1	chipotle pepper in adobo sauce, finely chopped	1
1 tsp	cumin seeds, toasted and ground (see Tip, left)	5 mL
1 lb	ground turkey	500 g
1	small onion, minced, about ½ cup (125 mL)	1
½ cup	dry bread crumbs	125 mL
1 tbsp	barbecue sauce	15 mL
1	egg, beaten	1
1 tsp	ground cumin	5 mL
½ tsp	salt	2 mL
	Freshly ground black pepper	
	Whole wheat hamburger buns	
	Sliced tomatoes, optional	
	Sliced Spanish or red onion, optional	
	Lettuce, optional	
	Sliced avocado or guacamole, optional	

1. *Chipotle Mayo:* In a bowl, combine mayonnaise, chipotle pepper and cumin. Stir until blended. Cover and refrigerate for 30 minutes to allow flavors to blend.

2. In a large bowl, combine ground turkey, onion, bread crumbs, barbecue sauce, egg, cumin, salt and pepper, to taste. Mix until well blended. Shape into 4 patties about the height of your rotisserie basket. Place in rotisserie basket, close lid tightly and load onto the spit rod assembly. Cook until the meat is no longer pink inside, about 25 minutes. Serve burgers on warm buns slathered with Chipotle Mayo and top with other garnishes as desired.

Variation
Chicken Burgers with Chipotle Mayo: Substitute ground chicken for the turkey.

Beef and Veal

When I was growing up, we often had roast beef for Sunday dinner. Now, for various reasons, roast beef has become a rare treat, which in some ways is unfortunate because it's truly delicious when cooked in a rotisserie oven. The constant rotation at moderate, even heat produces the juiciest and most succulent beef imaginable.

In my opinion, the best beef roasts to cook on the rotisserie are prime rib (with or without bones), top sirloin, tenderloin, and eye of round as long as it's well marbled. If you have a smaller oven, a bone-in prime rib roast may not fit, so check the manual that came with your machine to make certain your oven will accommodate a roast of this size. If so, run it through this preliminary test: load it onto the spit rods and test on the "no-heat rotation" setting to make sure it doesn't come in contact with any surface of the oven. If it does, you'll have to use boned and tied roasts in your oven.

The rotisserie also cooks fabulous flank steak — the best I've had — and great ground beef patties and meat loaves. Just be sure to use lean rather than extra-lean ground beef; the latter becomes overly dry as the fat drips off while cooking. I've also included recipes for short ribs, thick veal chops and a veal roast, all of which respond well to rotisserie cooking.

TEMPERATURE CHART FOR BEEF AND VEAL

Rare	140°F (60°C)
Medium	150°F (66°C)
Well done	170°F (77°C)

Be aware that due to carry-over cooking the internal temperature of a large roast will rise a few degrees between the time it is removed from the oven and carved. To ensure that your meat is not overcooked, remove it from the oven a few minutes before the internal temperature registers the desired degree of doneness.

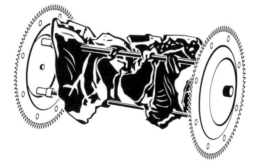

Bone-in veal chops
Spear the chops on the spit rods horizontally, ensuring they are evenly balanced and working around the bone to ensure they are secure. This may take a bit of wrangling.

Bone-in prime rib roast

Load meat onto the spit rods with rib bones parallel to the rods, ensuring it is evenly balanced (as shown in the diagram on the left). If the roast is placed off center, the rotisserie will not operate properly and the meat is likely to come in contact with the oven.

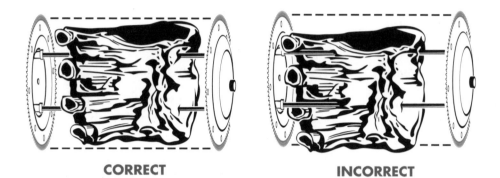

CORRECT   INCORRECT

Flank steak

Place the spit rod assembly in the rest area, if your model has one. Insert 3 kabob rods into the gear wheels with the spring ends on the left. Thread 2 kabob rods through the meat — one at the top and the other at the bottom — spacing them so they line up with holes on the gear wheels as well as the kabob rods that are already in place. Load rods onto the gear wheels with the spring ends on the left.

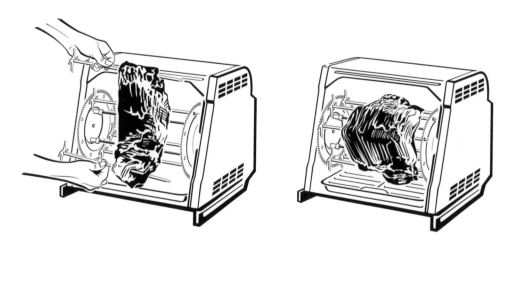

Basic Roast Beef

SERVES 6

Here is the basic technique for roasting a 3-pound (1.5 kg) boneless sirloin roast. You can vary the cut of beef to include other cuts, such as eye of round (see Rosemary Mustard–Coated Roast Beef, Step 3, page 61) or tenderloin (see Pancetta-Wrapped Tenderloin with Horseradish Cream, Step 4, page 65).

Tip

To crush coarse sea salt: Use a mortar and a pestle, or place the salt between 2 sheets of waxed paper and crush with a rolling pin or the bottom of a measuring cup. The salt should retain its chunky texture but be fine enough to rub evenly over the meat.

1	boneless beef sirloin roast, about 3 lbs (1.5 kg)	1
1 tbsp	coarse sea salt, lightly crushed (see Tip, left), or 1 tsp (5 mL) table salt	15 mL
	Freshly ground black pepper	
1 tbsp	olive oil	15 mL
	Horseradish, optional	

1. Pat roast dry with paper towel and rub all over with salt. Season with pepper, to taste. Brush with olive oil. Let stand at room temperature for 30 minutes to 1 hour.

2. When ready to roast, load meat onto the spit rods, ensuring it is evenly balanced. Roast until an instant-read thermometer inserted into the thickest part of the meat registers 150°F (66°C) for medium, about 50 minutes. Remove from spit rods, place on a warm platter and let rest for 10 minutes. Slice thinly and serve plain with horseradish, if using.

Variation

Instead of the sea salt mixture, rub the meat with seasoned salt, chili powder, Cajun seasoning or your favorite spice blend.

Flavored Butters

**MAKES ABOUT
1/2 CUP (125 ML) EACH**

Flavored butters make a nice finish for plain roasted fish, lamb or steak. If you prefer a smoother butter, press the mixture through a fine sieve after it has been blended.

Tip

You can also shape the blended butter into a roll, wrap in plastic wrap and refrigerate. When ready to use, cut it into 1/2-inch (1 cm) thick slices.

Sun-Dried Tomato Butter

1/2 cup	butter, at room temperature	125 mL
4	sun-dried tomatoes in oil, drained and diced	4
1 tbsp	snipped chives	15 mL
	Salt and freshly ground black pepper	

1. In a bowl, using a wooden spoon, beat butter until smooth and creamy. Add tomatoes, chives and salt and pepper, to taste. Mix until blended. (You can also do this in a mini-chopper, if you prefer.) Spoon into a ramekin or small bowl and chill until firm, about 30 minutes.

Roasted Red Pepper Butter

1/2 cup	butter, at room temperature	125 mL
1	roasted red pepper, peeled, seeded and diced	1
1 tsp	grated lemon zest	5 mL
	Salt and freshly ground black pepper	

1. In a bowl, using a wooden spoon, beat butter until smooth and creamy. Add pepper, lemon zest and salt and pepper, to taste. Mix until blended. (You can also do this in a mini-chopper, if you prefer.) Spoon into a ramekin or small bowl and chill for 2 hours or until ready to use.

Chipotle Butter

1/2 cup	butter, at room temperature	125 mL
2	chipotle peppers in adobo sauce	2
1/2 tsp	lime zest	2 mL
1 tsp	lime juice	5 mL
	Salt and freshly ground black pepper	

1. In a bowl, using a wooden spoon, beat butter until smooth and creamy. Add peppers, lime zest and juice and salt and pepper, to taste. Mix until blended. (You can also do this in a mini-chopper, if you prefer.) Spoon into a ramekin or small bowl and chill for 2 hours or until firm, about 30 minutes.

Double Mustard–Coated Prime Rib

SERVES 4 TO 6

In my opinion, bone-in prime rib is the king of roast beef, and you're not likely to have a better result than when it's roasted on a rotisserie. This is a classic preparation, and it works best with traditional accompaniments, such as oven-roasted potatoes, Yorkshire pudding and horseradish. Expect requests for seconds.

Tips

You will need a large rotisserie oven to roast a bone-in prime rib. If you have a smaller model, use these coatings for a 3-lb (1.5 kg) boneless roast and reduce cooking time to about 50 minutes for medium (see Basic Roast Beef, page 58, for detailed cooking instructions).

To crush coarse sea salt: Use a mortar and a pestle, or place the salt between 2 sheets of waxed paper and crush with a rolling pin or the bottom of a measuring cup. The salt should retain its chunky texture but be fine enough to rub evenly over the meat.

Large rotisserie oven

$\frac{1}{2}$ cup	Dijon mustard	125 mL
1 tbsp	yellow mustard seeds, optional	15 mL
1 tbsp	puréed garlic, 3 to 4 cloves (see Tips, page 30)	15 mL
1 tbsp	soy sauce	15 mL
1 tbsp	olive oil	15 mL
2 tsp	cracked black peppercorns	10 mL
1 tsp	coarse sea salt, lightly crushed (see Tips, left), or $\frac{1}{2}$ tsp (2 mL) table salt	5 mL
1	bone-in prime rib roast, about 5 lbs (2.5 kg)	1

1. In a small bowl, combine mustard, mustard seeds, if using, garlic, soy sauce, olive oil, peppercorns and salt.

2. Pat roast dry with paper towel. Spread with mustard mixture, ensuring that the surface is completely covered. Let stand at room temperature for 1 hour.

3. When ready to roast, load meat onto the spit rods with rib bones parallel to the rods, ensuring it is evenly balanced (see diagram, page 57). Roast until an instant-read thermometer inserted into the thickest part of the roast registers the desired degree of doneness, 150°F (66°C) for medium, about 1½ hours. Remove from spit rods and place on a warm platter. Cover loosely with foil and let rest for 10 minutes before carving.

Variation

Herb-Coated Prime Rib: In a small bowl, combine 2 tbsp (25 mL) each puréed garlic (6 to 8 cloves) and finely chopped fresh rosemary, 2 tsp (10 mL) each cracked black peppercorns and coarse sea salt, crushed, and 1 tbsp (15 mL) olive oil. Proceed with Step 2, substituting the herb mixture for the mustard.

Rosemary Mustard–Coated Roast Beef

SERVES 4

This classic coating works well with any beef roast as well as with lamb. At my butcher's suggestion, I tried a well-marbled eye of round, which he recommended specifically for a rotisserie oven. Although I was initially skeptical, believing as I did that eye of round can be a tad chewy, one try convinced me that he was right. If you're using this cut, my only caveat is to make sure the meat is well marbled — otherwise it's likely to be dry and perhaps not as tender as you would like.

Tips

When roasting a narrow roast such as eye of round, pay more attention to its width than to its weight when judging roasting times. A narrow roast takes about 16 minutes per pound (500 g) to reach medium-rare.

If you are using a different cut of beef, adjust the roasting times accordingly. Use an instant-read thermometer inserted into the thickest part of the meat to ensure it's done to suit your preference.

2 tbsp	Dijon mustard	25 mL
1 tbsp	coarse sea salt, lightly crushed (see Tips, page 60), or 1 tsp (5 mL) table salt	15 mL
1 tbsp	finely chopped rosemary leaves	15 mL
1 tbsp	puréed garlic, 3 to 4 cloves (see Tips, page 30)	15 mL
1 tsp	cracked black peppercorns	15 mL
1 tsp	dry mustard	15 mL
1	well-marbled eye of round roast or other cut suitable for roasting, about 2½ lbs (1.25 kg)	1
1 tbsp	olive oil	15 mL

1. In a small bowl, combine Dijon mustard, salt, rosemary, garlic, peppercorns and dry mustard.

2. Pat meat dry with paper towel. Brush with olive oil, ensuring the surface is entirely covered. Spread mustard mixture evenly over the meat. Let stand at room temperature for 30 minutes.

3. When ready to roast, load meat onto the spit rods, ensuring it is evenly balanced. Roast until an instant-read thermometer inserted into the thickest part of the meat registers the desired degree of doneness, 145°F (63°C) for medium-rare, about 40 minutes. Remove from spit rods, place on a warm platter and let rest for 10 minutes. Slice thinly and serve.

Peppery Roast Beef with Chimichurri Sauce

SERVES 4 TO 6

Chimichurri is a South American green sauce, traditionally served with churrasco-style grilled meats, most often steak. But I find it makes a great accompaniment for roast beef. Perhaps because of its Latin origins, I particularly enjoy this combination while dining alfresco on a lazy summer night. Add your favorite salad, a good bottle of Chilean Cabernet and enjoy!

Tip

You can also use ½ tsp (2 mL) ground cinnamon. Do not toast. Add to the spice mixture after it has been ground.

Chimichurri Sauce

2 cups	packed parsley leaves	500 mL
½	red bell pepper, coarsely chopped	½
1	long red chili or jalapeño pepper, chopped	1
2	cloves garlic, chopped	2
½ tsp	dried oregano leaves or 1 tbsp (15 mL) fresh oregano leaves	2 mL
½ tsp	salt	2 mL
½ tsp	freshly ground black pepper	2 mL
3 tbsp	red wine vinegar	45 mL
⅓ cup	extra virgin olive oil	75 mL

Spice Rub

1 tbsp	coarse sea salt or 1 tsp (5 mL) table salt	15 mL
1 tsp	cumin seeds	5 mL
2	dried red chili peppers	2
10	black peppercorns	10
¼ -inch	piece cinnamon stick (approx.) (see Tip, left)	0.5 cm
1	boneless beef roast, such as sirloin, prime rib or eye of round, about 3 lbs (1.5 kg)	1
1 tbsp	Asian chili oil or olive oil	15 mL

1. *Chimichurri Sauce:* In a food processor, combine parsley, bell pepper, chili pepper, garlic, oregano, salt, pepper and vinegar. Pulse until finely chopped. With motor running, gradually add olive oil through feed tube, processing until mixture is smooth. Cover and chill for about 2 hours to allow the flavors to blend.

2. *Spice Rub:* In a small dry skillet over medium heat, toast salt, cumin seeds, chilies, peppercorns and cinnamon until the spices release their aroma, about 2 minutes. Transfer to a spice grinder and grind to a fine powder. (You can also do this in a mortar with a pestle or between 2 sheets of waxed paper, using the bottom of a wine bottle or measuring cup.) Set aside.

3. Pat meat dry with paper towel. Rub spice mixture into the meat, covering all surfaces except for the ends. Brush with chili oil, ensuring the surface is entirely covered. Let stand at room temperature for 30 minutes.

4. When ready to roast, load meat onto the spit rods, ensuring it is evenly balanced. Roast until an instant-read thermometer inserted into the thickest part of the meat registers the desired degree of doneness, 145°F (63°C) for medium-rare, about 40 minutes. Remove from spit rods, place on a warm platter and let rest for 10 minutes. Slice thinly and serve accompanied with the sauce.

Variation

Mixed Peppercorn Crust: If you prefer, rub the beef with a simple mixture of sea salt and peppercorns. Skip the toasting step and combine 1 tbsp (15 mL) coarse sea salt with 1 tbsp (15 mL) each black, white and dried green peppercorns. Grind coarsely. Rub over the meat and brush with olive oil rather than chili oil. Continue as directed.

Indian-Spiced Roast Beef

SERVES 4 TO 6

This is a deliciously different way to serve roast beef. Serve with a mildly seasoned Indian pilaf and creamed spinach for a memorable meal.

Tips

I use a fine Microplane® grater when preparing garlic and gingerroot for rubs and coatings to be used on the rotisserie. It effectively purées the products, creating tiny particles that are completely integrated into the mixture. Larger particles are likely to fall off the meat as the rotisserie turns.

To crush coarse sea salt: Use a mortar and a pestle, or place the salt between 2 sheets of waxed paper and crush with a rolling pin or the bottom of a measuring cup. The salt should retain its chunky texture but be fine enough to rub evenly over the meat.

1/8 tsp	saffron threads	0.5 mL
1 tbsp	boiling water	15 mL
1 tbsp	coarse sea salt, lightly crushed (see Tips, left), or 1 tsp (5 mL) table salt	15 mL
1 tbsp	freshly squeezed lemon juice	15 mL
1 tbsp	plain yogurt	15 mL
1 tbsp	puréed gingerroot	15 mL
1 tbsp	puréed garlic, 3 to 4 cloves (see Tips, left)	15 mL
1 tbsp	garam masala	15 mL
1 tsp	yellow mustard seeds	5 mL
1/2 tsp	cracked black peppercorns	2 mL
1	boneless beef top sirloin roast, about 3 lbs (1.5 kg)	1

1. In a small bowl, dissolve saffron with 1 tbsp (15 mL) boiling water for 5 minutes.

2. Add salt, lemon juice, yogurt, gingerroot, garlic, garam masala, mustard seeds and peppercorns. Blend well.

3. Pat roast dry with paper towel. Spread spice paste evenly over the meat, being certain to completely cover the surface. Let stand at room temperature for 1 hour.

4. When ready to roast, load meat onto the spit rods, ensuring it is evenly balanced. Roast until an instant-read thermometer inserted into the thickest part of the meat registers the desired degree of doneness, 145°F (63°C) for medium-rare, about 50 minutes.

5. Remove meat from spit rods and place on a warm platter. Cover loosely with foil and let rest for 10 minutes. Slice thinly and serve.

Traditional Turkey Breast with Sage and Onion Stuffing (page 52)

Overleaf: Hoisin-Glazed Ribs (page 117)

Pancetta-Wrapped Tenderloin with Horseradish Cream

SERVES 4 TO 6

The tenderloin is, as its name suggests, the most tender part of the beef and, when properly roasted, it's succulent. Because it's so expensive, it's a rare treat. Its flavor is very mild and it has a tendency to dry out. Beef tenderloin is one of the few cuts that, in my opinion, should never be cooked beyond rare. I've found that letting it rest briefly in a salt rub before roasting enhances the flavor, as does wrapping it in pancetta, which also keeps it moist while roasting. The pancetta, a cured Italian bacon available in well-stocked supermarkets, crisps up while roasting and makes a nice accompaniment to the sliced meat. If you can't find it, substitute thinly sliced bacon.

Tip

The temperature of the meat will rise about 10°F (5°C) during the rest period due to carry-over cooking. If you want a truly rare tenderloin, you should remove it from the oven when the internal temperature registers 130°F (55°C).

1 tbsp	coarse sea salt, lightly crushed (see Tip, page 64), or 1 tsp (5 mL) table salt	15 mL
1 tsp	cracked black peppercorns	5 mL
1	beef tenderloin roast, about 3 lbs (1.5 kg)	1

Horseradish Cream

½ cup	whipping (35%) cream	125 mL
3 tbsp	prepared horseradish	45 mL
1 tsp	Dijon mustard	5 mL
2 tbsp	finely chopped chives	25 mL
6 oz	thinly sliced pancetta or bacon	175 g

1. In a small bowl, combine salt and peppercorns. Place the tenderloin on a plate large enough to accommodate it and rub all over with salt mixture. Cover with plastic wrap and let stand at room temperature for 1 hour.

2. *Horseradish Cream:* In a bowl, whisk cream until stiff. Add horseradish and mustard and whisk until blended. Fold in chives. Cover and refrigerate until ready to use, up to 1 hour.

3. Transfer meat to a work surface and wrap completely with pancetta, securing each piece with toothpicks. Tie the tenderloin with butcher's twine in 3 places along its length and once from end to end.

4. Load meat onto the spit rods, ensuring it is evenly balanced. Roast until an instant-read thermometer inserted into the thickest part of the meat registers the desired degree of doneness, 140°F (60°C) for rare, about 45 minutes (see Tip, left). Remove from spit rods and let rest for 10 minutes before carving. Serve with Horseradish Cream.

Double Mustard–Coated Prime Rib (page 60)

Rib Eye with Roquefort Butter

SERVES 2 TO 4

Because it's well marbled, a thick-cut rib eye steak can be successfully roasted on the rotisserie. I like to use the speed basket attachment on my rotisserie for this and to sear it for 2 minutes per side to facilitate browning. This produces a medium-rare steak. If you're using the regular basket, sear it for the required time and add about 5 minutes to the roasting time.

Tip

If you prefer, shape the blended butter into a roll, wrap in plastic wrap and refrigerate until firm, about 30 minutes. When ready to use, cut it into ½-inch (1 cm) thick slices.

Roquefort Butter

4 oz	Roquefort cheese	125 g
¼ cup	butter, at room temperature	50 mL
1	clove garlic, minced	1
1 tsp	Worcestershire sauce	5 mL
1	boneless beef rib eye steak, 1 inch (2.5 cm) thick, about 1½ lbs (750 g)	1

1. *Roquefort Butter:* In a bowl, using a wooden spoon, beat cheese and butter until smooth and creamy. Add garlic and Worcestershire sauce and mix until blended. (You can also do this in a mini-chopper, if you prefer.) Spoon into a ramekin or small bowl and chill until firm, about 30 minutes.

2. Place steak in the speed basket (see Tips, left), close lid tightly and load onto the spit rod assembly. Roast in the B position for 12 minutes. Position the basket so one side of the steak is facing the heating coils and press the "pause to sear" setting. Roast for 2 minutes. Repeat with the other side of the meat. Remove from basket and transfer to a cutting board. Let rest for 5 minutes. Slice thinly and serve with Roquefort Butter.

> **Variation**
> Substitute another butter, such as Sun-Dried Tomato, Roasted Red Pepper or Chipotle (see recipes, page 59), for the Roquefort Butter.

Korean-Style Beef Kabobs

SERVES 4 TO 6

I never tire of this simple combination of flavors. I love the hot pepper juxtaposed with the sweetness of the sugar and the rich sesame oil, but if heat doesn't appeal to you, omit the chili pepper. The results are still delicious.

Tip

I use a fine Microplane® grater when preparing garlic for rubs and coatings to be used on the rotisserie. It effectively purées the garlic, creating tiny particles that are completely integrated into the mixture. Larger particles are likely to fall off the meat as the rotisserie turns.

½ cup	soy sauce	125 mL
1 tbsp	sesame oil	15 mL
1 tbsp	puréed garlic, 3 to 4 cloves (see Tip, left)	15 mL
1 tsp	cracked black peppercorns	5 mL
1 tsp	granulated sugar	5 mL
1	long red chili pepper, minced, optional	1
1	boneless beef top sirloin steak, 1 inch (2.5 cm) thick, about 2 lbs (1 kg)	1
12	small white mushrooms	12
12	large green onions, white part only	12
1	red bell pepper, cut into 1-inch (2.5 cm) squares	1
1	yellow bell pepper, cut into 1-inch (2.5 cm) squares	1

1. In a large bowl, combine soy sauce, sesame oil, garlic, peppercorns, sugar and chili pepper, if using. Stir well. Trim fat from beef and cut into 1-inch (2.5 cm) cubes. Add beef to soy mixture and toss until well coated. Cover and marinate at room temperature for 1 hour or in the refrigerator for 4 to 6 hours.

2. Remove beef from marinade and pat dry with paper towel. Discard marinade. Thread beef onto the kabob rods, alternating with mushrooms, onions and red and yellow peppers, leaving space between the pieces to allow the heat to circulate. Load rods onto the gear wheels with spring ends on the right, or according to the manufacturer's instructions for rotation. Roast until the beef reaches the desired degree of doneness, about 15 minutes for medium. Remove from the skewers and serve immediately.

Portuguese Beef Brochettes

SERVES 4 TO 6

These beef brochettes, known as espetada *in Portugal, consist of chunks of sirloin rubbed with sea salt and garlic and served with a dense, moist bread that is a regional specialty. I adapted this recipe from one that appeared in* **Saveur** *magazine. It suggested substituting English muffins for the specialty bread, which, true to its rustic roots, makes a great casual dinner with friends. Each diner cuts his or her roasted meat into bite-size pieces and wraps it in bits of muffin. Serve this with a sliced tomato salad and an abundance of robust red wine for a very convivial meal.*

Tips

Because the meat is coated in salt, I prefer to roast it in chunks that are larger than I normally use for brochettes. This reduces the ratio of salt to meat. Diners can cut each piece into bite-size morsels before eating.

Brochettes

1	boneless beef top sirloin steak, 2 inches (5 cm) thick, about 2 lbs (1 kg)	1
2 tbsp	olive oil	25 mL
2 tsp	piri-piri sauce (see Tips, right)	10 mL
1 tbsp	coarse sea salt, lightly crushed (see Tips, right), or 1 tsp (5 mL) table salt	15 mL
1 tbsp	puréed garlic, 3 to 4 cloves (see Tips, page 67)	15 mL
4	bay leaves, crumbled	4

Muffins with Lemon Parsley Butter

1/2 cup	butter, at room temperature	125 mL
1/4 cup	finely chopped parsley	50 mL
2 tsp	puréed garlic, about 2 cloves	10 mL
1/4 tsp	grated lemon zest	1 mL
1 tbsp	freshly squeezed lemon juice	15 mL
	Freshly ground black pepper	
4 to 6	English muffins (preferably whole wheat), toasted	4 to 6

1. *Brochettes:* Trim fat from steak and cut into 2-inch (5 cm) cubes (see Tips, left). Pat dry with paper towel. In a small bowl, combine olive oil and piri-piri sauce. Brush evenly over beef, ensuring that all surfaces are completely covered.

2. On a plate, combine salt, garlic and bay leaves. Roll beef in the mixture until it is evenly coated. Let stand at room temperature for 30 minutes.

To crush coarse sea salt: Use a mortar and a pestle, or place the salt between 2 sheets of waxed paper and crush with a rolling pin or the bottom of a measuring cup. The salt should retain its chunky texture but be fine enough to rub evenly over the meat.

Piri-piri sauce is a hot pepper sauce with a unique flavor that is popular in Portugal. It's made from a very hot pepper grown in Africa. It's available in specialty food stores, but if you can't find it, use your favorite hot pepper sauce instead.

Sea salt has a milder, sweeter flavor than table salt, which can leave a bitter aftertaste. Although this seems like a lot of salt, some drips off while the meat is roasting. If is it still too salty for you, scrape off the excess before eating.

3. When ready to roast, thread meat onto the kabob rods, leaving space between the pieces to allow the heat to circulate. Load rods onto the gear wheels with the spring ends on the right, or according to the manufacturer's instructions for rotation. Roast until the beef reaches the desired degree of doneness, about 20 minutes for medium. Remove from skewers and serve immediately.

4. *Muffins with Lemon Parsley Butter:* In a bowl, using a wooden spoon, beat butter until smooth and creamy. Add parsley, garlic, lemon zest and juice and pepper, to taste. Mix until blended. (You can also do this in a mini-chopper, if you prefer.) Spread over hot toasted English muffins and serve alongside the brochettes.

Beef Fajitas

SERVES 4 TO 6

Fajitas are a fun solution to the perennial problem of what to have for dinner. Kids love rolling them up and adding their own fixins'. These are fairly mild, but if your family likes a bit of spice, include the hot banana pepper.

Tips

If you can't find New Mexico chili powder, use ancho or regular chili powder in this recipe.

Achiote seeds, also known as annatto, have a mild peppery flavor and can easily be ground in a mortar or a spice grinder. They are often used in Mexican and Latin American cooking and are usually available in supermarkets that have a well-stocked spice department. If you can't find them, paprika makes a satisfactory substitute.

1	boneless beef top sirloin steak, 1 inch (2.5 cm) thick, about 2 lbs (1 kg)	1
1 tbsp	New Mexico chili powder (see Tips, left)	15 mL
2 tsp	cumin seeds, toasted and ground (see Tips, right)	10 mL
1 tsp	ground achiote seeds or paprika	5 mL
½ tsp	freshly ground black pepper	2 mL
2 tbsp	olive oil, divided	25 mL
1	red bell pepper, cut into 1-inch (2.5 cm) cubes	1
1	green bell pepper, cut into 1-inch (2.5 cm) cubes	1
8	large green onions, white part only	8
1	whole hot banana pepper, optional	1
	Sea salt	
	Freshly squeezed lime juice	
	Extra virgin olive oil	
6	large tortillas	6
	Salsa	
	Chopped tomato, optional	
	Sliced avocado, optional	
	Finely chopped cilantro, optional	
	Sour cream, optional	

1. Pat meat dry with paper towel and trim off any fat. In a bowl, combine chili powder, cumin, achiote seeds and black pepper. Rub onto both sides of meat. Brush with 1 tbsp (15 mL) olive oil. Let stand at room temperature for 30 minutes. Cut meat into 1-inch (2.5 cm) cubes.

To toast cumin seeds: Place seeds in a dry skillet over medium heat and cook, stirring, until they release their aroma and just begin to brown, 3 to 4 minutes. Immediately transfer to a spice grinder or a mortar and grind.

2. Brush red and green peppers and green onions lightly with remaining olive oil. On separate kabob rods, skewer the meat, bell peppers, green onions and hot pepper, if using, leaving space between the individual pieces to allow the heat to circulate. Insert the rods into the gear wheels with the spring ends on the right, or according to the manufacturer's instructions for rotation. Cook until meat reaches the desired degree of doneness, about 15 minutes for medium. (If you prefer your vegetables more tender, remove the meat and continue cooking the veggies to desired doneness.)

3. Slide the meat onto one plate and the bell peppers and green onions onto another. Finely chop the banana pepper, if using, and place in a small dish. Season the meat with sea salt and drizzle with lime juice. Drizzle olive oil over the vegetables.

4. To serve, give each guest a tortilla. Pass the meat, vegetables and condiments and let them help themselves.

Easy Tacos

SERVES 6

Here's a great family dinner that is a hit with kids and adults alike. It's a meal in itself and is quite nutritious with the full range of accompaniments.

Tip

To toast cumin seeds: Place seeds in a dry skillet over medium heat and cook, stirring, until they release their aroma and just begin to brown, 3 to 4 minutes. Immediately transfer to a spice grinder or a mortar and grind.

1 tsp	grated orange zest	5 mL
½ cup	freshly squeezed orange juice	125 mL
¼ tsp	grated lime zest	1 mL
¼ cup	freshly squeezed lime juice	50 mL
1 tbsp	chili powder	15 mL
2 tsp	cumin seeds, toasted and ground (see Tip, left)	10 mL
¼ tsp	ground allspice	1 mL
3 tbsp	olive oil	45 mL
1	flank steak, 1½ to 2 lbs (750 g to 1 kg)	1
6	medium tortillas, warmed	6
	Salsa	
	Shredded lettuce	
	Finely chopped green onion	
	Roasted bell peppers, optional	
	Sliced avocado drizzled with lime juice, optional	

1. In a bowl, combine orange zest and juice, lime zest and juice, chili powder, cumin and allspice. Stir to blend. Whisk in oil.

2. Score flank steak on the diagonal in 3 places on each side. Place in a long shallow non-reactive dish large enough to lay it flat. Pour half the marinade over the steak. Turn and repeat. Cover and marinate in the refrigerator at least 4 hours or overnight.

3. When ready to cook, remove meat from the marinade and pat dry with paper towel. Discard marinade. Thread 2 kabob rods through the meat — one at the top and the other at the bottom — spacing them so they line up with the holes on the gear wheels (see diagram, page 57). Load rods onto the gear wheels with the spring ends on the left, or according to the manufacturer's instructions for stability. Cook for 25 minutes for medium. Remove the kabob rods and place meat on a warm platter. Let rest for 5 minutes.

4. Cut steak thinly on the diagonal and arrange in the middle of each tortilla. Top with salsa and accompaniments.

Pineapple Soy Flank Steak

SERVES 4

Flank steak is one of my favorite cuts of beef because it's so flavorful. The problem is it needs a tenderizing marinade to counteract its inherent chewiness, and it can easily dry out when barbecued. That's why I'm so excited by the results I've achieved in the rotisserie oven. The longer, slower cooking distributes the juices and produces the moistest, most succulent flank steak I've ever had. Try this — it's simple and absolutely delicious!

Tip

I use a fine Microplane® grater when preparing garlic and gingerroot for rubs and coatings to be used on the rotisserie. It effectively purées the products, creating tiny particles that are completely integrated into the mixture. Larger particles are likely to fall off the meat as the rotisserie turns.

1 cup	unsweetened pineapple juice	250 mL
1/2 cup	soy sauce	125 mL
2 tbsp	puréed garlic, 6 to 8 cloves (see Tip, left)	25 mL
1 tbsp	puréed gingerroot	15 mL
1	long red chili pepper, minced, optional	1
1	flank steak, 1 1/2 to 2 lbs (750 g to 1 kg) Coarsely ground sea salt, optional	1

1. In a bowl, combine pineapple juice, soy sauce, garlic, gingerroot and chili pepper, if using.

2. Score flank steak on the diagonal in 3 places on each side. Place in a long shallow non-reactive dish large enough to lay it flat. Pour half the marinade over the steak. Turn and repeat. Cover and marinate in the refrigerator for at least 4 hours or overnight.

3. When ready to cook, remove meat from the marinade and pat dry with paper towel. Discard marinade. Thread 2 kabob rods through the meat — one at the top and the other at the bottom — spacing them so they line up with the holes on the gear wheels (see diagram, page 57). Load rods onto the gear wheels with the spring ends on the left, or according to the manufacturer's instructions for stability. Cook for 25 minutes for medium. Remove the kabob rods and place meat on a warm platter. Sprinkle with sea salt, if using. Let rest for 5 minutes. Slice thinly across the grain on the diagonal.

Flank Steak Dijon

SERVES 4

This is an easy way of preparing flank steak: it's marinated in a simple vinaigrette and then, after roasting, accented with a Dijon mustard finish. Serve this with oven-roasted potatoes and steamed broccoli for a great family meal.

Tip

For convenience, you can marinate the steak in ¾ cup (175 mL) of your favorite bottled oil and vinegar dressing instead of the garlic, vinegar and olive oil vinaigrette.

4	cloves garlic, minced	4
½ cup	olive oil	125 mL
3 tbsp	red wine vinegar	45 mL
1	flank steak, 1½ to 2 lbs (750 g to 1 kg)	1
1 tsp	Dijon mustard	5 mL
1 tbsp	extra virgin olive oil	15 mL
	Coarsely ground sea salt and freshly ground black pepper	

1. In a long shallow dish large enough to accommodate the flank steak or in a resealable plastic bag, combine garlic, olive oil and vinegar.

2. Pat steak dry with paper towel and score on the diagonal in 3 places on each side. Add to marinade, turning the steak several times to ensure it is well coated. Cover and marinate in the refrigerator for at least 4 hours or overnight.

3. When ready to cook, remove steak from the marinade. Discard marinade. Thread 2 kabob rods through the meat — one at the top and the other at the bottom — spacing them so they line up with the holes on the gear wheels (see diagram, page 57). Load rods onto the gear wheels with the spring ends on the left, or according to the manufacturer's instructions for stability. Roast for 25 minutes for medium. Remove the kabob rods and place meat on a warm platter.

4. In a small bowl, combine mustard and olive oil. Pour over steak. Season with sea salt and pepper, to taste. Let rest for 5 minutes. Slice meat thinly across the grain on the diagonal.

Red-Eye Flank Steak

SERVES 4

Nobody quite knows where red-eye gravy got its name, but this tasty concoction, traditionally a pan-fried ham steak smothered in a coffee-based gravy, is an old favorite in the Deep South. In recent years, contemporary chefs looking to add unique flavors to main-course dishes have picked up on this idea and have begun to use coffee as a seasoning for meat. This recipe was inspired by one developed by Gordon Hamersley, the chef at Boston's highly esteemed restaurant Hamersley's Bistro. The deep, rich coffee flavors of the marinade are a delightful complement to the succulent steak.

Tip

I prefer to use coarse sea salt in this recipe and lightly crush it in a mortar with a pestle or on a cutting board, using the bottom of a wine bottle or measuring cup. You can also use an equal quantity of kosher salt or ¼ tsp (1 mL) table salt.

1 cup	strong brewed black coffee	250 mL
2	cloves garlic, minced	2
2 tbsp	coarse-grain mustard	25 mL
2 tbsp	balsamic or sherry vinegar	25 mL
3 tbsp	packed brown sugar	45 mL
1 tbsp	olive oil	15 mL
1 tsp	cracked black peppercorns	5 mL
½ tsp	coarse sea salt, lightly crushed (see Tip, left), or kosher salt	2 mL
¼ tsp	cayenne pepper	1 mL
1	flank steak, 1½ to 2 lbs (750 g to 1 kg)	1
	Coarsely ground sea salt, optional	

1. In a bowl, combine coffee, garlic, mustard, vinegar, brown sugar, olive oil, peppercorns, salt and cayenne. Pour off ¼ cup (50 mL) of the mixture. Cover and refrigerate.

2. Score flank steak on the diagonal in 3 places on each side. Place in a long shallow dish large enough to lay it flat. Pour half the remaining marinade over the steak. Turn and repeat with the rest. Cover and marinate in the refrigerator for at least 4 hours or overnight.

3. When ready to cook, remove steak from the marinade and pat dry with paper towel. Discard marinade. Thread 2 kabob rods through the meat — one at the top and the other at the bottom — spacing them so they line up with the holes on the gear wheels (see diagram, page 57). Load rods onto the gear wheels with the spring ends on the left, or according to the manufacturer's instructions for stability. Cook for 25 minutes for medium. Remove the kabob rods and place meat on a warm platter. Sprinkle with sea salt, if using, and let rest for 5 minutes. Pour reserved marinade over steak. Slice thinly across the grain on the diagonal.

Stuffed Flank Steak

SERVES 4

Not only is this tasty, but when sliced it makes a particularly pretty presentation. This recipe, which is Latin American in origin, is traditionally made with butterflied steak, but I find that slicing it into two distinct pieces on the horizontal works better for a rotisserie oven because the two smaller rolls fit neatly into the rotisserie basket.

Tips

It's not that hard to cut a flank steak in half on the horizontal. You need a sharp knife with a long thin blade. Place the meat on a cutting board and, holding it steady with one hand, cut through it on the horizontal, folding the top part open as you cut. If you want to butterfly it, stop short of the end and open it up.

If you prefer, you can make one big roll by butterflying the steak (don't cut through it completely). Roll up as described, tie crosswise in 4 places and lengthwise twice. Load the roll onto the spit rods, securing with string, if necessary, and roast until an instant-read thermometer inserted into the thickest part of the meat registers 150°F (66°C) for medium, about 50 minutes.

2 tbsp	freshly squeezed lemon juice	25 mL
1 tsp	herbes de Provence	5 mL
1 tsp	minced garlic	5 mL
½ tsp	salt	2 mL
⅓ cup	olive oil	75 mL
1	flank steak, 1½ to 2 lbs (750 g to 1 kg), sliced in half horizontally (see Tips, left)	1

Stuffing

4	drained oil-packed sun-dried tomatoes, minced	4
4	cloves roasted garlic, mashed (see recipe, page 148)	4
¼ cup	finely chopped parsley	50 mL
2	roasted red peppers, peeled and thinly sliced (see recipe, page 155)	2

1. In a small bowl, combine lemon juice, herbes de Provence, garlic and salt. Stir until salt has dissolved. Whisk in olive oil. Spread about 1 tbsp (15 mL) of the mixture on each side of the steak halves, rubbing it into the meat. Place steak in a shallow dish just large enough to accommodate it and pour remaining mixture over the meat. Turn several times to ensure all the surfaces are well coated. Cover and refrigerate for 6 hours or overnight.

2. *Stuffing:* In a bowl, combine sun-dried tomatoes, roasted garlic and parsley. Transfer one piece of steak from the marinade to a cutting board. Spread with half the tomato mixture, then arrange half the peppers evenly over mixture, laying them on the vertical.

3. Starting with one long edge of the meat closest to you, roll up the steak like a jelly roll, securing with 3 toothpicks. With butcher's string and starting in the middle of the roll, tie tightly in 4 different places along the length, then make one tie from end to end. Remove toothpicks and discard. Repeat with second steak, discarding marinade. Place the rolls in the rotisserie basket, close lid tightly and load onto the spit rod assembly. Cook until an instant-read thermometer inserted into the thickest part of the meat registers 150°F (66°C) for medium, about 40 minutes. Slice thinly across the grain and serve.

Spicy Asian Patties

SERVES 4

Highly spiced ground meat patties are a tradition in many countries. This version is distinguished by Asian seasonings and makes a particularly tasty accompaniment to stir-fried vegetables. If you prefer, shape the meat into oblongs rather than patties and serve it as a wrap in lettuce leaves (see Variation).

Tips

Unless you are on a low-fat diet, I recommend using lean rather than extra-lean ground beef when making patties on the rotisserie. Because the fat melts and drips away during roasting, patties made from extra-lean ground beef are quite dry when roasted on the rotisserie.

Don't confuse Asian chili sauce with tomato-based chili sauce, which is often substituted for ketchup. The Asian version, which is available in many supermarkets as well as Asian markets, is made from ground chilies and is very spicy. It often has garlic added.

1 lb	lean ground beef	500 g
1	egg, lightly beaten	1
2 tbsp	Worcestershire sauce	25 mL
2 tbsp	ketchup	25 mL
1 tbsp	minced garlic	15 mL
1 tbsp	soy sauce	15 mL
1 tbsp	Asian chili sauce (see Tips, left)	15 mL
1/2 tsp	salt	2 mL
1/2 tsp	cracked black peppercorns	2 mL
1/2 cup	dry bread crumbs	125 mL

1. In a large bowl, combine beef, egg, Worcestershire sauce, ketchup, garlic, soy sauce, chili sauce, salt, peppercorns and bread crumbs and mix thoroughly.

2. Shape into 4 uniformly sized patties about the height of your rotisserie basket. Place in a single layer in the rotisserie basket, close lid tightly and load onto the spit rod assembly. Cook until meat is no longer pink inside, about 25 minutes. Serve immediately.

Variation

Spicy Beef Wraps: When mixed, shape the meat into 8 to 12 oblong patties and reduce the cooking time to 20 minutes. When the meat is cooked, place each patty on a leaf of iceberg lettuce. Garnish with crisp bean sprouts and sprinkle with chopped roasted peanuts, if desired. Fold the lettuce over to form a wrap.

Italian-Style Burgers with Crispy Crumb Topping

SERVES 4 TO 6

Here's another great recipe for meat patties, this time with an Italian flair. The combination of onion and sage with a garlic-flavored crumb topping is quite delectable. I like to serve this with stir-fried rapini tossed with olive oil, lemon juice and garlic, and a sliced tomato salad, in season.

Tip

Unless you are on a low-fat diet, I recommend using lean rather than extra-lean ground beef when making patties on the rotisserie. Because the fat melts and drips away during roasting, patties made from extra-lean ground beef are quite dry when roasted on the rotisserie.

1	large onion, coarsely chopped	1
20	fresh sage leaves	20
3/4 tsp	salt	4 mL
	Freshly ground black pepper	
1 1/2 lbs	lean ground beef (see Tip, left)	750 g
1	egg, beaten	1
1/4 cup	freshly grated Parmesan cheese	50 mL
1 1/4 cups	dry bread crumbs, divided	300 mL
1 tbsp	butter	15 mL
1 tsp	minced garlic	5 mL

1. In a food processor, combine onion, sage, salt and pepper. Pulse until the mixture is very finely chopped and blended. Add beef, egg, Parmesan and 1/4 cup (50 mL) bread crumbs and pulse until combined.

2. Shape into 4 to 6 uniformly sized patties about the height of your rotisserie basket. Place in a single layer in the rotisserie basket, close lid tightly and load onto the spit rod assembly. Cook until the meat is no longer pink inside, about 25 minutes.

3. In a skillet, melt butter over medium heat. Add garlic and cook, stirring, until softened, about 1 minute. Add remaining 1 cup (250 mL) bread crumbs and cook, stirring, until golden brown, about 6 minutes. To serve, place burgers on a warm platter and top with bread crumbs.

Best-Ever Cheeseburgers

SERVES 4 TO 6

Here's the solution for days when nothing but flavorful, juicy cheeseburgers will do. Serve them with a tossed green salad for a great family meal and add some robust red wine for a casual dinner with friends.

1 ½ lbs	lean ground beef (see Tip, page 78)	750 g
1	small onion, finely chopped	1
1 tbsp	dried Italian seasoning	15 mL
1 tbsp	Worcestershire sauce	15 mL
4	cloves garlic, minced	4
¾ tsp	salt	4 mL
1	egg, beaten	1
	Freshly ground black pepper	
	Whole wheat hamburger buns	
	Sliced Cheddar cheese	
	Sliced tomatoes	
	Dijon mustard	
	Thinly sliced red onion	

1. In a large bowl, combine beef, onion, Italian seasoning, Worcestershire sauce, garlic, salt, egg and pepper, to taste. Mix until well blended.

2. Shape into 4 to 6 uniformly sized patties about the height of your rotisserie basket. Place in a single layer in the rotisserie basket, close lid tightly and load onto the spit rod assembly. Cook until meat is no longer pink inside, about 25 minutes.

3. Preheat broiler. Cut buns in half and toast lightly under the broiler on a baking sheet. Lay cheese and sliced tomatoes on the bottom half and broil until the cheese starts to melt. (You want it to be melted but not running over the sides.) Set a burger patty on top of melted cheese, slather with mustard and top with an onion slice and remaining bun.

Korean-Style Short Ribs

SERVES 4

Short ribs are one of my favorite cuts of meat because they are so flavorful. The problem is that they are also very fatty and, unless properly cooked, rather tough. This Asian marinade tenderizes the ribs, and cooking them on the rotisserie eliminates unwanted fat while producing delicious results.

Tips

Crosscut short ribs, sometimes known as flanken, are shorter and meatier than beef ribs that are cut in a rack. I like to cut them into individual pieces before cooking as it allows all sides of the meat to be coated with the marinade, adding flavor and tenderizing.

If adding fresh chili peppers as a garnish, Thai bird's eye or long red or green chilies work best in this recipe.

Marinade

½ cup	soy sauce	125 mL
2 tbsp	rice vinegar	25 mL
1 tbsp	minced garlic	15 mL
1 tbsp	minced gingerroot	15 mL
1 tbsp	sesame oil	15 mL
1 tbsp	granulated sugar	15 mL
1 tsp	cracked black peppercorns	5 mL
3 lbs	crosscut beef short ribs (see Tips, left)	1.5 kg
2 tbsp	toasted sesame seeds (see Tips, page 32)	25 mL
2 tbsp	finely chopped green onion and/or fresh chili peppers	25 mL

1. *Marinade:* In a bowl, combine soy sauce, rice vinegar, garlic, gingerroot, sesame oil, sugar and peppercorns.

2. Cut ribs into individual pieces and place in a large bowl or resealable plastic bag. Add the marinade and toss well to ensure the meat is thoroughly coated. Cover and refrigerate overnight.

3. Drain off the marinade and discard. Arrange ribs in the rotisserie basket, close lid tightly and load onto the spit rod assembly. Cook until cooked through, about 1 hour.

4. Transfer to a large platter and sprinkle with sesame seeds, green onions and/or chili peppers.

Tuscan-Style Veal Chops

SERVES 4

This couldn't be simpler, yet it's an extremely elegant dish. A seared veal chop is complemented with the barest of additions — extra virgin olive oil, freshly ground black pepper and freshly squeezed lemon juice. Use your best olive oil and, if you feel the need to dress it up, sprinkle the meat with finely chopped parsley or rosemary as soon as you take it off the rotisserie.

Tips

If you prefer, roast the chops in the rotisserie basket. If you have a speed basket attachment and the chops will fit, use it for this recipe.

Cook chops in the B position and reduce cooking time by about 5 minutes.

4	bone-in rib veal chops, 1 inch (2.5 cm) thick (each about 12 oz/375 g)	4
	Coarse sea salt	
2 tbsp	finely chopped rosemary leaves or parsley, optional	25 mL
	Freshly ground black pepper	
¼ cup	extra virgin olive oil	50 mL
2 tbsp	freshly squeezed lemon juice	25 mL

1. Pat meat dry with paper towel and sprinkle both sides liberally with salt. Cover and let stand at room temperature for 30 minutes.

2. Thread chops onto the spit rods on the horizontal, working around the bone to ensure they are secure. (This may take a bit of wrangling. See diagram, page 56). Roast until an instant-read thermometer inserted into the thickest part of the meat registers 150°F (66°C) for medium, about 30 minutes.

3. Remove the chops from the spit rods and place on a warm platter. Sprinkle with rosemary, if using, and pepper, to taste. Drizzle with olive oil and lemon juice. Let rest for 5 minutes, then serve.

Spicy Roast Veal

SERVES 6 TO 8

Although roast veal is not a common cut, it makes a pleasant change from beef. Serve this with Marinated Roasted Peppers (see recipe, page 156) to inspire a Mediterranean mood.

1	boneless veal shoulder roast, about 3 lbs (1.5 kg)	1
¼ cup	finely chopped parsley	50 mL
1 tsp	finely grated lemon zest	5 mL
1 tsp	freshly squeezed lemon juice	5 mL
2 to 3	cloves garlic, thinly sliced	2 to 3
¼ cup	Dijon mustard	50 mL
1 tbsp	extra virgin olive oil	15 mL
½ tsp	cayenne pepper	2 mL

1. Pat roast dry with paper towel and make 10 deep slits in the meat, evenly distributed from end to end and on both sides.

2. In a small bowl, combine parsley and lemon juice. Stuff each slit with one slice of garlic and parsley mixture.

3. In a separate bowl, combine mustard, olive oil, lemon zest and cayenne. Brush evenly over the roast, covering all surfaces. Let stand at room temperature for 30 minutes to 1 hour.

4. Load roast onto the spit rods, ensuring it is evenly balanced. Roast until an instant-read thermometer inserted into the thickest part of the meat registers 150°F (66°C) for medium, about 50 minutes.

5. Remove from the spit rods and let rest for 10 minutes before carving.

Lamb and Pork

If you enjoy eating lamb or pork, you'll love the results you get when you roast it in your rotisserie oven. The meat, which cooks from the outside in, is juicier than when cooked by other methods. Because much of the unwanted fat melts off, you can feel positive about making healthy changes to your diet.

The best cuts of lamb for the rotisserie are leg and rack roasts, chops, and cut-up leg, which makes delicious kabobs. You can roast a bone-in leg of lamb in the large rotisserie — just ask your butcher to break the bone and tie it for you, and try it out on the "no-heat rotation" setting to make sure no part is coming in contact with the machine. You should also check it several times while it's roasting to make sure the twine securing the bone hasn't loosened. If it has, stop the machine and retie it.

Pork roasts, rolled and tied, and bone-in rib roasts also do very well in the rotisserie, and I'd be hard pressed to cook pork chops any other way. I find that chops become dry on the barbecue or when pan-fried, but if you take the time to brine them before roasting, they are positively succulent on the rotisserie. You can also make delicious kabobs and ribs. Although pork does need to be cooked until just a hint of pink remains in the center of the meat, be careful not to overcook it. When the internal temperature reaches 160°F (71°C), it's done.

TEMPERATURE CHART FOR LAMB

Rare	140°F (60°C), about 12 minutes/lb (26 minutes/kg)
Medium	150°F (66°C), about 15 minutes/lb (33 minutes/kg)
Well done	170°F (77°C), about 22 minutes/lb (48 minutes/kg)

TEMPERATURE CHART FOR PORK

Medium-well	160°F (71°C)
Boneless pork double-loin roast, about 3 lbs (1.5 kg), about 1 hour and 20 minutes	
Boneless pork single-loin roast, about 3 lbs (1.5 kg), 50 to 60 minutes	
Bone-in pork loin roast, about 5 lbs (2.5 kg), about 1 hour and 45 minutes	

Be aware that due to carry-over cooking, the internal temperature of a large lamb or pork roast will rise a few degrees between the time it is removed from the oven and carved. To ensure that your meat is not overcooked, remove it from the oven a few minutes before the internal temperature registers the desired degree of doneness.

Rack of baby lamb

Spear each rack on one spit rod. Use a kabob rod, woven through the bones and inserted into the gear wheel with the spring end on the left, to hold it in place.

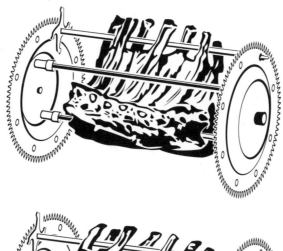

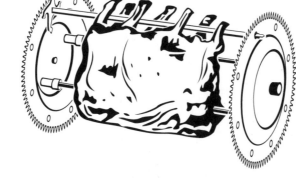

Lamb chops

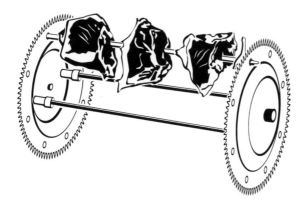

Thread chops onto kabob rods, about 3 to a rod, avoiding the bone and leaving space between each to allow the heat to circulate. Load rods onto the gear wheels with the spring ends on the right, placing a rod in every second hole.

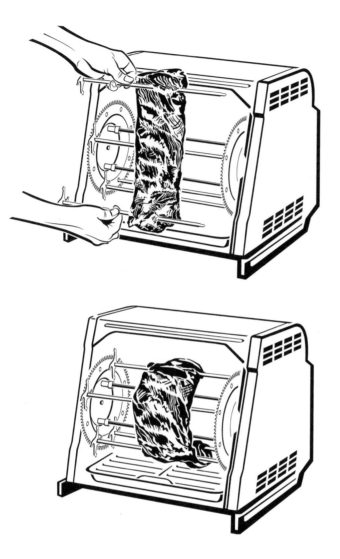

Ribs

Place the spit rod assembly in the rest area, then insert 3 kabob rods into the gear wheels with the spring ends on the left. Thread 2 kabob rods through the ribs — one at the top and the other at the bottom — spacing them so they line up with the holes on the gear wheels as well as the kabob rods that are already in place. If you are cooking a second rack of ribs, repeat, threading the second piece of meat so you have both racks side by side on 2 kabob rods. Load rods onto the gear wheels with the spring ends on the left.

Mustard-Coated Leg of Lamb

SERVES 6 TO 8

This is a variation on Julia Child's recipe for Herb and Mustard Coated Leg of Lamb. The first time I ever cooked a leg of lamb (with great trepidation for a dinner party), I followed her recipe to a T and the results were superb. For many years, her recipe became my preferred method for cooking leg of lamb, and this version still produces outstanding results in the rotisserie oven.

Tip

You can also make this recipe using a 3-lb (1.5 kg) boned, rolled leg of lamb instead. Roast until an instant-read thermometer inserted into the thickest part of the roast registers 145°F (63°C), about 45 minutes for medium-rare.

Large rotisserie oven

1	leg of lamb, about 4 lbs (2 kg), bone-in, broken at the joint and tied tightly (see Tip, page 88)	1
4	cloves garlic, cut into slivers	4
2 tbsp	finely chopped rosemary leaves	25 mL
1/4 cup	Dijon mustard	50 mL
2 tbsp	soy sauce	25 mL
2 tbsp	yellow mustard seeds	25 mL
1 tbsp	olive oil	15 mL

1. With a sharp knife, cut slashes all over the meat, about 1/2 inch (1 cm) deep, and stuff each with a sliver of garlic and a pinch of rosemary.

2. In a small bowl, combine Dijon mustard, soy sauce, mustard seeds and olive oil. Brush mixture over meat, ensuring that the surfaces are completely covered. Let stand at room temperature for 1 hour.

3. Load lamb onto the spit rods, ensuring that it is evenly balanced. Roast until an instant-read thermometer inserted into the thickest part of the leg registers 145°F (63°C) for medium-rare, about 1 hour. Remove from spit rods and transfer to a warm platter. Let rest for 5 minutes before carving.

Wine-Marinated Leg of Lamb

SERVES 6 TO 8

Leg of lamb is one of my favorite dishes for a dinner party or festive family gathering. It's simple but elegant, and roasted on the rotisserie it is particularly succulent. Serve with the optional wine gravy or, for convenience, bottled mint sauce or tomato chutney. Add Pot-Roasted New Potatoes (see recipe, page 103) and creamed spinach to complete the meal.

Tips

To roast a bone-in leg of lamb on the rotisserie, have your butcher break the bone at the joint and tie it tightly. Before starting to roast, position the meat on the spit rods and rotate for 1 minute on the "no-heat rotation" setting to make sure that it's not making contact with any part of the oven. If necessary, remove the lamb from the spit rods and reposition it. Also, check the meat a few times while it is roasting to make certain the string holding the bone in place hasn't slackened. If so, stop the rotisserie and retie it.

Large rotisserie oven

1	leg of lamb, about 4 lbs (2 kg), bone-in, broken at the joint and tied tightly (see Tips, left)	1
4	cloves garlic, cut into slivers	4
2 tbsp	finely chopped rosemary leaves	25 mL
2 cups	dry red wine	500 mL
1 tbsp	coarse sea salt, crushed (see Tips, right), or 1 tsp (5 mL) table salt	15 mL
1 tsp	dry mustard	5 mL
½ tsp	cracked black peppercorns	2 mL
Pinch	ground allspice	Pinch
1 tbsp	olive oil	15 mL

Red Wine Sauce, optional

	Reserved marinade	
1 tbsp	olive oil	15 mL
2 tbsp	finely chopped shallots	25 mL
1 tbsp	all-purpose flour	15 mL
¼ cup	concentrated beef consommé	50 mL

1. With a sharp knife, cut slashes all over the meat, about ½ inch (1 cm) deep, and stuff each with a sliver of garlic and a pinch of rosemary. Place lamb in a flat-bottomed dish and pour the wine over the meat. (You can also do this in a large resealable plastic bag.) Cover with plastic wrap and marinate overnight in the refrigerator, turning several times and spooning the wine over the meat each time.

2. Remove meat from marinade and pat dry with paper towel. Reserve the marinade if you are planning to make Red Wine Sauce.

You can also make this recipe using a 3-lb (1. 5 kg) boned, rolled leg of lamb instead. Roast until an instant-read thermometer inserted into the thickest part of the roast registers 145°F (63°C), about 45 minutes for medium-rare.

To crush coarse sea salt: Use a mortar and a pestle, or place the salt between 2 sheets of waxed paper and crush with a rolling pin or the bottom of a measuring cup. The salt should retain its chunky texture but be fine enough to rub evenly over the meat.

3. In a small bowl, combine salt, mustard, peppercorns and allspice. Rub the mixture into the meat. Brush with olive oil, ensuring that all surfaces are covered.

4. Load lamb onto the spit rods, ensuring that it is evenly balanced. Roast until an instant-read thermometer inserted into the thickest part of the leg registers 145°F (63°C) for medium-rare, about 1 hour. Remove from spit rods and transfer to a warm platter. Let rest for 5 minutes before carving. If making sauce, pour the cooking juices from the drip tray into a small bowl and set aside.

5. *Red Wine Sauce:* In a saucepan over medium heat, bring reserved marinade to a boil. Reduce heat to low and simmer until it has reduced by half, about 10 minutes. Remove from heat and set aside.

6. In another saucepan, heat olive oil over medium heat. Add shallots and cook, stirring, until softened, about 3 minutes. Add flour and cook, stirring, for 1 minute. Add any juices that have accumulated from the resting roast, the reduced marinade and beef consommé and cook, stirring, until slightly thickened, about 3 minutes. Pour into a sauceboat and serve alongside the sliced lamb.

Butterflied Leg of Lamb with Anchovy Olive Stuffing

SERVES 4 TO 6

Roast lamb, anchovies and olives make a particularly mouth-watering combination. I like to serve this with Easy Pine Nut Pilaf (see recipe, page 99) and slightly crisp green beans tossed with butter and a few drops of lemon juice.

Tip

To crush coarse sea salt: Use a mortar and pestle, or place the salt between 2 sheets of waxed paper and crush with a rolling pin or the bottom of a measuring cup.

2 tbsp	olive oil	25 mL
1 tbsp	freshly squeezed lemon juice	15 mL
2	cloves garlic, minced	2
1 tsp	coarse sea salt, crushed (see Tip, left), or ½ tsp (2 mL) table salt	5 mL
1 tsp	cracked black peppercorns	5 mL
1	butterflied leg of lamb, about 3 lbs (1.5 kg), unrolled	1

Anchovy Olive Stuffing

1½ cups	pitted black olives	375 mL
½ cup	packed parsley leaves	125 mL
8	anchovy fillets	8
2	cloves garlic, minced	2
2	sun-dried tomatoes in olive oil	2
½ tsp	grated lemon zest	2 mL

1. In a small bowl, combine olive oil, lemon juice, garlic, sea salt and peppercorns. Spread lamb flat on a cutting board and rub half the mixture over the inside of the meat. Pour remainder into a shallow dish. Roll up the lamb, place in dish and roll until the surface is completely covered with the marinade. Cover and let stand at room temperature for 1 hour.

2. *Anchovy Olive Stuffing:* In a food processor, combine olives, parsley, anchovies, garlic, sun-dried tomatoes and lemon zest. Unroll lamb and spread mixture evenly over the inside of the meat. Roll up like a jelly roll and tie securely with butcher's twine in 3 places along the length of the meat and once from end to end.

3. Load lamb onto the spit rods, ensuring it is evenly balanced. Roast until an instant-read thermometer inserted into the thickest part of the meat registers 155°F (66°C) for medium, about 50 minutes. Remove from spit rods and transfer to a warm platter. Let rest for 5 minutes before carving.

Three-Pepper Lamb Chops with Mint Glaze

SERVES 4 TO 6

These tasty chops are delicious enough to serve to guests yet so easy to make you can enjoy them for a weekday meal.

Tip

Some rotisserie ovens come with an accessory called a speed basket, which cooks in the B position, closer to the heat source. If you have this accessory and the chops will fit, by all means use it for cooking lamb chops as they will brown more effectively than when cooked in the regular position.

1 tbsp	coarse sea salt, crushed (see Tip, page 90), or 1 tsp (5 mL) table salt	15 mL
1 tbsp	ancho chili powder	15 mL
2 tsp	cracked black peppercorns	10 mL
12	loin lamb chops, 1 inch (2.5 cm) thick, about 2½ lbs (1.25 kg)	12

Mint Glaze

½ cup	mint jelly	125 mL
2 tsp	Asian chili sauce, such as sambal oelek	10 mL

1. In a bowl, combine salt, chili powder and peppercorns. Rub spice mixture into both sides of lamb chops. Let stand at room temperature for 30 minutes.

2. *Mint Glaze:* In a saucepan over medium heat, combine mint jelly and chili sauce. Cook, stirring, until mixture is melted and blended, about 1 minute. Spoon half the mixture into a small bowl and set aside.

3. Thread chops onto 4 kabob rods, avoiding the bone and leaving space between each chop to allow the heat to circulate (see diagram, page 85). Load rods onto the gear wheels with the spring ends on the right, or according to the manufacturer's instructions for rotation, placing a rod in every second hole. Roast for 10 minutes, then stop the machine and brush both sides of each chop liberally with jelly mixture. Reset the timer and continue roasting until an instant-read thermometer inserted into the thickest part of the meat registers 145°F (63°C) for medium-rare, about 15 minutes longer. Serve reserved Mint Glaze alongside.

Rosemary Garlic Lamb Chops

SERVES 4 TO 5

The combination of rosemary and garlic is a classic French seasoning for lamb. These flavorful chops make a great weeknight dinner, accompanied by parsleyed new potatoes and sliced tomatoes with vinaigrette. Roast them on the kabob rods or in the rotisserie basket, whichever you prefer (see Tip, below).

Tip

Lamb chops are small enough to roast on the kabob rods, which, in my opinion is the preferred method as they brown more evenly. However, they can also be roasted in the rotisserie basket, which is more convenient. If you roast them in the basket and find they have not browned enough after 20 minutes, position the basket so one side is facing the heating coils and press the "pause to sear" setting.

2 tsp	whole black peppercorns	10 mL
1 tbsp	coarse sea salt or 1 tsp (5 mL) table salt	15 mL
1 tbsp	finely chopped rosemary leaves	15 mL
2 tsp	minced garlic	10 mL
1 tbsp	olive oil	15 mL
10	loin lamb chops, 1 inch (2.5 cm) thick, about 2 lbs (1 kg)	10
1 cup	dry red wine (approx.)	250 mL

1. Place peppercorns on a sheet of waxed paper or in a mortar. Using a rolling pin or a pestle, crush until peppercorns are quite cracked. Add salt and continue crushing until the pepper is well cracked and the salt is still a bit chunky, if using coarse sea salt. Transfer to a small bowl. Add rosemary, garlic and olive oil. Stir well until combined.

2. Pat lamb chops dry with paper towel. Rub salt mixture into both sides of the chops. Place chops in a shallow dish just large enough to accommodate them in a single layer. Add wine just to cover. (You can also do this in a resealable plastic bag.) Cover and refrigerate for at least 2 hours or overnight.

3. Thread chops onto 3 to 4 kabob rods, avoiding the bone and leaving space between each chop to allow the heat to circulate (see diagram, page 85). Load rods onto the gear wheels with the spring ends on the right, or according to the manufacturer's instructions for rotation. Roast until an instant-read thermometer inserted into the thickest part of the meat registers 150°F (66°C) for medium, about 25 minutes. Remove from kabob rods and serve.

Indian-Spiced Lamb Chops

SERVES 4 TO 5

The Indian spicing in this recipe is a nice change. I like to serve this with Easy Pine Nut Pilaf (see recipe, page 99) and puréed spinach. I discovered the affinity between tomato chutney and lamb chops many years ago, when I spent a delightful weekend at the Old Drover's Inn in Dover Plains, New York. At that time, their signature dish was grilled lamb chops with tomato chutney, and it was delicious! But if you don't have tomato chutney in your pantry, these tasty chops can stand on their own.

Tip

Some rotisserie ovens come with an accessory called a speed basket, which cooks in the B position, closer to the heat source. If you have this accessory and the chops will fit, by all means use it for cooking lamb chops as they will brown more effectively than when cooked in the regular position.

¼ cup	plain yogurt	50 mL
1 tbsp	puréed garlic, 3 to 4 cloves (see Tips, page 101)	15 mL
1 tbsp	puréed gingerroot	15 mL
1 tsp	black cardamom seeds, ground	5 mL
1 tsp	cumin seeds, toasted and ground (see Tips, page 97)	5 mL
10	loin lamb chops, 1 inch (2.5 cm) thick, about 2 lbs (1 kg)	10
1 tsp	paprika	5 mL
⅛ tsp	cayenne pepper	0.5 mL
	Tomato chutney, optional	

1. In a shallow dish just large enough to accommodate the lamb in a single layer or in a resealable plastic bag, combine yogurt, garlic, gingerroot, cardamom and cumin. Add lamb chops and toss until thoroughly coated. Cover and refrigerate for 4 hours or overnight.

2. Remove lamb from marinade and pat dry with paper towel. Discard marinade. Sprinkle lamb with paprika and cayenne. Let stand at room temperature for 30 minutes.

3. Thread chops onto 3 to 4 kabob rods, avoiding the bone and leaving space between each chop to allow the heat to circulate (see diagram, page 85). Load rods onto the gear wheels with the spring ends on the right, or according to the manufacturer's instructions for rotation. Roast until an instant-read thermometer inserted into the thickest part of the meat registers 150°F (66°C) for medium, about 25 minutes. Remove from kabob rods and serve with tomato chutney, if desired.

Rack of Lamb with Greek Stuffing

SERVES 4

Here's a recipe that gives you all the élan of a rack of lamb with the benefit of a stuffing. Of course, it's not really stuffing — it's a variation of the Greek sauce skordalia, made with bread instead of the more usual mashed potatoes. Serve each piece of lamb with a dollop of the tasty mixture and savor the delicious combination.

Tips

A rack of lamb is a rib roast. I've specified French-cut because the long bones look so elegant, but for the purposes of this recipe, any rack of lamb will do. Just be sure to roast it to the proper internal temperature.

Although all lamb is, by definition, less than one year old, the size of a rack will vary depending upon the age of the animal. A rack of baby lamb, which is less than four months old, is too small to fit on both spit rods. Therefore, I recommend spearing each rack with one grill rod and using a kabob rod, woven through the bones and inserted into the gear wheel with the spring ends on the left, to hold it in place, or according to the manufacturer's instructions for stability.

1 tsp	coarse sea salt or ½ tsp (2 mL) table salt	5 mL
1 tsp	dried oregano leaves	5 mL
½ tsp	cracked black peppercorns	2 mL
1 tbsp	olive oil	15 mL
1 tsp	grated lemon zest	5 mL
2	French-cut racks of baby lamb, each about 1½ lbs (750 g) (see Tips, left), or 1 rack of lamb, about 4 lbs (2 kg) (see Tips, page 98)	2

Greek Stuffing

2	slices country-style bread, about 1 inch (2.5 cm) thick, crusts removed	2
¼ cup	water	50 mL
¼ cup	coarsely chopped blanched almonds, toasted	50 mL
1 tbsp	minced garlic	15 mL
2 tbsp	freshly squeezed lemon juice	25 mL
¼ tsp	fine salt, preferably fine sea salt	1 mL
⅓ cup	extra virgin olive oil	75 mL
	Freshly ground black pepper	

1. In a mortar or a spice grinder, combine sea salt, oregano and peppercorns. Lightly grind until oregano is relatively fine and the salt is still chunky but adequately crushed, if using coarse sea salt, so it will adhere to the meat. Transfer to a small bowl. Add olive oil and lemon zest and stir to blend.

2. Pat meat dry with paper towel. Rub salt mixture all over the surface, pressing into the meat. Load onto the spit rods (see Tips, left, and diagram, page 85). Roast until an instant-read thermometer inserted into the thickest part of the meat registers 145°F (63°C) for medium-rare, about 30 minutes for baby lamb or 1 hour and 10 minutes for a large (4 lb/2 kg) rack. Remove from the spit rods and transfer to warm platter. Let rest for 5 minutes.

Be aware that some French-cut racks of lamb have extremely long bones. If you are cooking 2 racks simultaneously, they may come in contact with the heat source during rotation, due to the position of the spit rods. If this happens during testing, remove the offending rack from the spit rod and skewer it on a kabob rod instead. Insert that kabob rod (spring end on the left) farther along the gear wheel than the spit rod so that when you thread the second rod through the bones to hold them in place, they do not come in contact with any part of the oven.

3. *Greek Stuffing:* In a bowl, combine bread and water. Squeeze out water, ensuring the bread is well moistened, then transfer to a food processor. Add almonds, garlic, lemon juice and salt and process until relatively smooth. With motor running, add olive oil in a steady stream through the feed tube, processing until smooth. Season with pepper, to taste.

4. To serve, slice lamb into individual chops and spoon a dollop of the Greek Stuffing over each one.

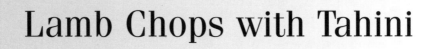

Lamb Chops with Tahini

SERVES 4 TO 5

Tasty and oh so easy to make, these chops are Middle Eastern in their sensibility. Serve them with couscous to extend the mood.

Tips

Lamb chops are small enough to roast on the kabob rods, which in my opinion is the preferred method as they brown more evenly. However, they can also be roasted in the rotisserie basket, which is more convenient. If you roast them in the basket and find they have not browned enough after 20 minutes, position the basket so one side is facing the heating coils and press the "pause to sear" setting.

To crush coarse sea salt: Use a mortar and a pestle, or place the salt between 2 sheets of waxed paper and crush with a rolling pin or the bottom of a measuring cup. The salt should retain its chunky texture but be fine enough to rub evenly over the meat.

1 tbsp	puréed garlic, 3 to 4 cloves (see Tips, page 101)	15 mL
1 tsp	coarse sea salt, crushed (see Tips, left), or ½ tsp (2 mL) table salt	5 mL
½ tsp	hot paprika	2 mL
½ tsp	ground cumin	2 mL
1 tbsp	olive oil	15 mL
10	loin lamb chops, 1 inch (2.5 cm) thick, about 2 lbs (1 kg)	10

Tahini Sauce

1 tbsp	tahini	15 mL
1 tbsp	hot water	15 mL
1 tbsp	freshly squeezed lemon juice	15 mL

1. In a bowl, combine garlic, salt, paprika, cumin and olive oil. Rub spice mixture into both sides of lamb chops. Cover with plastic wrap and let stand at room temperature for 30 minutes.

2. Thread chops onto 3 to 4 kabob rods, avoiding the bone and leaving space between each chop to allow the heat to circulate (see diagram, page 85). Load rods onto the gear wheels with the spring ends on the right, or according to the manufacturer's instructions for rotation. Roast until an instant-read thermometer inserted into the thickest part of the meat registers 150°F (66°C) for medium, about 25 minutes. Remove from kabob robs and serve.

3. *Tahini Sauce:* In a bowl, combine tahini, hot water and lemon juice. Serve alongside the lamb.

Beef Fajitas (page 70)

Overleaf: Parsley Lemon Shrimp (page 142) with Aïoli (page 140)

Peppery Lamb Chops

SERVES 4 TO 5

The combination of spices in this simple treatment really brings out the flavor of the lamb.

Tips

Some rotisserie ovens come with an accessory called a speed basket, which cooks in the B position, closer to the heat source. If you have this accessory and the chops will fit, by all means use it for cooking lamb chops as they will brown more effectively than when cooked in the regular position.

To toast cumin seeds: Place seeds in a dry skillet over medium heat and cook, stirring, until they release their aroma and just begin to brown, 3 to 4 minutes. Immediately transfer to a spice grinder or a mortar and grind.

1 tbsp	cumin seeds, toasted and ground (see Tips, left)	15 mL
1 tbsp	puréed garlic, 3 to 4 cloves (see Tips, page 101)	15 mL
1 tsp	dried oregano leaves	5 mL
½ tsp	cracked black peppercorns	2 mL
10	loin lamb chops, 1 inch (2.5 cm) thick, about 2 lbs (1 kg)	10
1 tbsp	olive oil	15 mL
	Sea salt	

1. In a small bowl, combine cumin, garlic, oregano and peppercorns.

2. Pat lamb dry with paper towel. Rub spice mixture into both sides of lamb chops. Brush with olive oil. Cover with plastic wrap and let stand at room temperature for 30 minutes.

3. Thread chops onto 3 to 4 kabob rods, avoiding the bone and leaving space between each chop to allow the heat to circulate (see diagram, page 85). Load rods onto the gear wheels with the spring ends on the right, or according to the manufacturer's instructions for rotation. Roast until an instant-read thermometer inserted into the thickest part of the meat registers 150°F (66°C) for medium, about 25 minutes. Remove from kabob rods. Sprinkle with salt and serve.

Red-Eye Flank Steak (page 75)

Rack of Baby Lamb with Green Sauce

SERVES 4

This dish is delicious any time of the year, but I particularly enjoy eating it in the summer, when fresh greens are abundant and at their peak. Look for sorrel, which has a bitter but refreshing bite, in farmer's markets or in the herb section of well-stocked supermarkets. I like to serve this with Easy Pine Nut Pilaf (see recipe, page 99) and a robust red wine such as rioja.

Tips

You can also make this recipe using a larger rack of lamb, about 4 lbs (2 kg). Load it onto the spit rods and roast until the internal temperature reaches 145°F (63°C) for medium-rare, about 1 hour and 10 minutes.

The roasting times for a rack of lamb will vary depending upon its circumference. Be sure to use an instant-read thermometer inserted into the thickest part of the meat to check the internal temperature. It should read 140 to 160°F (60 to 71°C), depending upon how well done you like your meat.

1 tbsp	puréed garlic, 3 to 4 cloves (see Tips, page 101)	15 mL
2 tsp	grated lemon zest	10 mL
1 tsp	coarse sea salt, crushed (see Tips, page 96), or ½ tsp (2 mL) table salt	5 mL
1 tsp	cracked black peppercorns	5 mL
1 tsp	dry mustard	5 mL
2	French-cut racks of baby lamb, each about 1½ lbs (750 g) (see Tips, page 94), or 1 rack of lamb, about 4 lbs (2 kg) (see Tips, left)	2
1 tbsp	olive oil	15 mL

Green Sauce

2	slices baguette, each about 1 inch (2.5 cm) thick, crusts removed	2
2 tbsp	freshly squeezed lemon juice	25 mL
2 cups	tightly packed arugula leaves	500 mL
1 cup	tightly packed parsley leaves	250 mL
1 cup	tightly packed sorrel leaves (see Tip, page 99)	250 mL
2	cloves garlic, chopped	2
4	anchovy fillets	4
½ tsp	fine salt, preferably sea salt	2 mL
½ cup	extra virgin olive oil	125 mL
	Freshly ground black pepper	

1. In a small bowl, combine garlic, lemon zest, salt, peppercorns and mustard.

2. Pat lamb dry with paper towel. Rub garlic mixture over the surface, excluding the end pieces and pressing into the meat. Brush the entire roast with olive oil, including the end pieces. Cover with plastic wrap and let stand at room temperature for 30 minutes.

Be aware that some French-cut racks of lamb have extremely long bones. If you are cooking 2 racks simultaneously, they may come in contact with the heat source during rotation, due to the position of the spit rods. If this happens during testing, remove the offending rack from the spit rod and skewer it on a kabob rod instead. Insert that kabob rod (spring end on the left) farther along the gear wheel than the spit rod so that when you thread the second rod through the bones to hold them in place, they do not come in contact with any part of the oven.

Make an effort to find sorrel as its flavorful bite enhances this sauce. But if you're not successful, use an additional cup (250 mL) arugula instead.

3. *Green Sauce:* In a bowl, combine baguette and lemon juice. Squeeze to ensure the bread is saturated with the juice, then transfer to a food processor. Add arugula, parsley, sorrel, garlic, anchovies and salt and process until blended. With motor running, add olive oil in a steady stream through the feed tube, processing until mixture is smooth and blended. Season with pepper, to taste, and add more salt, if necessary. Cover and refrigerate for at least 1 hour to allow flavors to blend.

4. Load meat onto the spit rods (see Tips, page 94, and diagram, page 85). Roast until an instant-read thermometer inserted into the thickest part of the meat registers 145°F (63°C) for medium-rare, about 30 minutes for baby lamb or 1 hour and 10 minutes for a larger (4 lb/2 kg) rack. Remove from the spit rods and transfer to a warm platter. Let rest for 5 minutes.

5. Slice into individual chops and serve with Green Sauce on the side.

Easy Pine Nut Pilaf

1. In a cast-iron pot with a tight-fitting lid, bring 1 cup (250 mL) long-grain rice, such as basmati, and 2 cups (500 mL) chicken stock to a rolling boil. Cover tightly, turn off heat and let sit on element for 20 minutes. (This works best on an electric stove.) Meanwhile, in a small skillet, melt 1 tbsp (15 mL) butter over medium heat. Add 2 tbsp (25 mL) pine nuts and cook, stirring, until lightly browned. Immediately remove from heat. When rice is cooked, add toasted pine nuts. Stir well and season with freshly ground black pepper, to taste, and serve.

Lamb Souvlaki

SERVES 4 TO 6

This classic Greek dish makes a great casual meal. To continue the Greek theme, I like to serve it with a Greek salad and hot orzo tossed with olive oil and sprinkled with feta.

Tips

You will need 2½ to 3 lbs (1.25 to 1.5 kg) boneless lamb leg to get 2 lbs (1 kg) of 1-inch (2.5 cm) cubes.

You can also make this recipe with lamb shoulder. You will need about double the amount of untrimmed lamb shoulder (about 4 lbs/2 kg) to trim and cut to get enough cubes for this recipe. If trimmed and cubed lamb is available from your butcher or meat counter, it is worthwhile to buy and save time and waste.

1 tsp	grated lemon zest	5 mL
2 tbsp	freshly squeezed lemon juice	25 mL
½ cup	dry white wine	125 mL
4	cloves garlic, minced	4
1 tsp	dried oregano leaves	5 mL
2	bay leaves, crumbled	2
½ tsp	fine sea salt or table salt	2 mL
¼ tsp	freshly ground black pepper	1 mL
¼ cup	olive oil	50 mL
2 lbs	boneless lamb leg, trimmed and cut into 1-inch (2.5 cm) cubes (see Tips, left)	1 kg
1	red bell pepper, cut into 1-inch (2.5 cm) cubes	1
1	red onion, cut into 8 wedges, then separated	1

1. In a shallow dish large enough to accommodate the lamb or in a resealable plastic bag, combine lemon zest and juice, white wine, garlic, oregano, bay leaves, salt and pepper. Stir well until salt dissolves. Whisk in olive oil. Add lamb pieces and toss to coat. Cover and marinate in the refrigerator for at least 6 hours or preferably overnight.

2. When ready to roast, thread lamb, pepper and onion alternately onto the kabob rods. Load rods onto the gear wheels with the spring ends on the right, or according to the manufacturer's instructions for rotation. Roast for about 20 minutes for medium-rare.

> **Variation**
> *Souvlaki in Pita:* Serve in warm pita bread with tomato slices, shredded lettuce and tzatziki (see recipe, page 36, or use a prepared version).

Italian-Style Pork Roast with Fennel

SERVES 6

The flavors in this dish are intriguingly different and delicious. To complement the seasoning and continue the Italian theme, accompany this with hot polenta.

Tips

If you prefer, substitute 3 tbsp (45 mL) fresh rosemary, finely chopped, for the dried. Add to the spice mixture along with the garlic.

You can also make this recipe with a 5-lb (2.5 kg) bone-in pork loin roast. Roast until an instant-read thermometer inserted into the thickest part of the meat registers 160°F (71°C), about 1 hour and 45 minutes.

I use a fine Microplane® grater when preparing garlic for rubs and coatings to be used on the rotisserie. It effectively purées the products, creating tiny particles that are completely integrated into the mixture. Larger particles are likely to fall off the meat as the rotisserie turns.

1 tbsp	dried rosemary leaves (see Tips, left)	15 mL
1 tbsp	fennel seeds	15 mL
1 tsp	cracked black peppercorns	5 mL
1 tbsp	coarse sea salt or 1 tsp (5 mL) table salt	15 mL
3 tbsp	puréed garlic, 9 to 12 cloves (see Tips, left)	45 mL
1	boneless pork double-loin roast, about 3 lbs (1.5 kg), trimmed and tied, or 1 boneless pork single-loin roast, about 3 lbs (1.5 kg), trimmed and tied (see Tips, left)	1

1. In a mortar with a pestle or between waxed paper and using the bottom of a measuring cup, crush rosemary, fennel seeds and peppercorns until they begin to powder but are still a bit chunky. Add salt and crush lightly. Transfer to a small bowl. Add garlic and mix to combine.

2. Pat pork dry with paper towel. Rub herb mixture into the meat, covering the entire surface. Cover with plastic wrap and let stand at room temperature for 1 hour or place in a large dish, cover and refrigerate overnight.

3. Load meat onto the spit rods, ensuring it is evenly balanced. Roast until an instant-read thermometer inserted into the thickest part of the meat registers 160°F (71°C), about 1 hour and 20 minutes for the double-loin roast (depending upon the diameter of your roast, wider roasts may take longer), and 50 to 60 minutes for the single-loin roast. Let rest for 5 minutes before carving.

Salt-Rubbed Pork Roast with Almond Cherry Sauce

SERVES 6 TO 8

If you don't want to make the Almond Cherry Sauce, this traditionally seasoned pork is delicious on its own. I like to serve this with puréed spinach and Pot-Roasted New Potatoes (see recipe, page 103) tossed with chives.

Tips

Substitute ¼ tsp (1 mL) ground allspice if you prefer.

You can also make this recipe with a 5-lb (2.5 kg) bone-in pork loin roast. Roast until an instant-read thermometer inserted into the thickest part of the meat registers 160°F (71°C), about 1 hour and 45 minutes.

I use a fine Microplane® grater when preparing garlic for rubs and coatings to be used on the rotisserie. It effectively purées the garlic, creating tiny particles that are completely integrated into the mixture. Larger particles are likely to fall off the meat as the rotisserie turns.

¼ tsp	whole allspice	1 mL
1 tsp	black peppercorns	5 mL
1 tbsp	coarse sea salt (see Tips, right) or 1 tsp (5 mL) table salt	15 mL
1 tsp	dried thyme leaves	5 mL
1 tsp	dry mustard	5 mL
2 tbsp	puréed garlic, 6 to 8 cloves (see Tips, left)	25 mL
1	boneless pork double-loin roast, about 3 lbs (1.5 kg), trimmed and tied, or 1 boneless pork single-loin roast, about 3 lbs (1.5 kg), trimmed and tied (see Tips, left)	1

Almond Cherry Sauce

1 cup	cherry preserves	250 mL
2 tbsp	balsamic vinegar	25 mL
1 tsp	grated orange zest	5 mL
¼ cup	toasted almonds, coarsely chopped, optional	50 mL

1. In a mortar with a pestle, crush allspice to a powder. Add peppercorns and crush until they are cracked. Add salt and crush coarsely. Transfer to a small bowl. Add thyme leaves, mustard and garlic and stir to combine. Rub mixture all over pork. Cover with plastic wrap and let stand at room temperature for 1 hour.

2. Load meat onto the spit rods, ensuring it is evenly balanced. Roast until an instant-read thermometer inserted into the thickest part of the meat registers 160°F (71°C), about 1 hour and 20 minutes for the double-loin roast (depending upon the diameter of your roast, wider roasts may take longer), and 50 to 60 minutes for the single-loin roast. Let rest for 5 minutes before carving.

I prefer the clean, crisp taste and enhanced mineral content of sea salt over refined table salt, which has a bitter, acrid taste. I always have plenty of sea salt on hand in my kitchen, but you can use tiny quantities of table salt in its place, if you prefer.

3. *Almond Cherry Sauce:* In a saucepan over low heat, combine cherry preserves, balsamic vinegar and orange zest. Cook, stirring occasionally, until preserves dissolve. Stir in almonds, if using. Pass separately at the table, along with the sliced pork.

Pot-Roasted New Potatoes

1. In a cast-iron pot with a tight-fitting lid, melt 1 to 2 tbsp (15 to 25 mL) butter. Add $\frac{1}{2}$ tsp (2 mL) coarsely ground sea salt (or $\frac{1}{4}$ tsp/1 mL table salt) and 6 to 10 small new potatoes. Toss to ensure the potatoes are well coated with the butter mixture. Cover, reduce heat to low and cook until the potatoes are tender when pierced with a fork, shaking the pot several times, about 25 minutes. Add 2 tbsp (25 mL) chopped chives or green onions to the pot. Stir well. Season with pepper, to taste, and serve.

Roasted Jamaican Jerked Pork

SERVES 6 TO 8

Although I love Jamaican jerk seasoning, I find it can be a bit overpowering on small pieces of meat. The advantage to using it to season a roast is that the ratio of meat to seasoning is increased, which means that even people who may be a bit spice averse will enjoy the rich island flavors. This is very tasty by itself, but if you like to gild the lily, as I sometimes do, add the Pineapple Salsa.

Tips

I prefer to use 1 tsp (5 mL) whole allspice in this recipe and to grind it in a mortar with a pestle just before using as the freshly ground flavor is more intense.

If you prefer, use a mini-chopper to make the jerk marinade. Crush the spices and coarsely chop the green onions, garlic, peppers and gingerroot. Add the remaining ingredients and process until smooth.

2 tsp	coarse sea salt, crushed, or 1 tsp (5 mL) table salt	10 mL
1 tsp	cracked black peppercorns	5 mL
½ tsp	ground allspice (see Tips, left)	2 mL
½ tsp	ground cinnamon	2 mL
4	green onions, white part only, minced	4
4	cloves garlic, minced	4
2	habanero or Scotch bonnet peppers, minced	2
1 tbsp	minced gingerroot	15 mL
3 tbsp	freshly squeezed lime juice	45 mL
1 tbsp	olive oil	15 mL
1 tbsp	soy sauce	15 mL
1	boneless pork double-loin roast, about 3 lbs (1.5 kg), trimmed and tied, or 1 boneless pork single-loin roast, about 3 lbs (1.5 kg), trimmed and tied	1

Pineapple Salsa

2 cups	cubed (½ inch/1 cm) pineapple	500 mL
½	red bell pepper, diced	½
1	jalapeño pepper, minced	1
4	green onions, minced	4
1	clove garlic, minced	1
1 tsp	minced gingerroot	5 mL
2 tbsp	freshly squeezed lime juice	25 mL
2 tbsp	finely chopped cilantro	25 mL

1. In a small bowl, combine sea salt, peppercorns, allspice, cinnamon, green onions, garlic, peppers, gingerroot, lime juice, olive oil and soy sauce.

2. Pat pork dry with paper towel. Rub spice mixture into the meat, covering the entire surface. Place in a large dish, cover and refrigerate overnight.

You can also make this recipe with a 5-lb (2.5 kg) bone-in pork loin roast. Roast until an instant-read thermometer inserted into the thickest part of the meat registers 160°F (71°C), about 1 hour and 45 minutes.

3. Load meat onto the spit rods, ensuring it is evenly balanced. Roast until an instant-read thermometer inserted into the thickest part of the meat registers 160°F (71°C), about 1 hour and 20 minutes for the double-loin roast (depending upon the diameter of your roast, wider roasts may take longer), and 50 to 60 minutes for the single-loin roast. Let rest for 5 minutes before carving.

4. *Pineapple Salsa:* Meanwhile, in a bowl, combine pineapple, red pepper, jalapeño pepper, green onions, garlic, gingerroot, lime juice and cilantro. Let stand at room temperature for 30 minutes or covered in the refrigerator for up to 6 hours to blend flavors. Serve alongside the sliced pork.

Chili-Roasted Loin of Pork with Apricot Chipotle Stuffing

SERVES 6 TO 8

Although it's a bit of work to untie then retie a rolled pork roast, adding a stuffing is one way of enhancing the preparation for a special meal. I love this apricot-chipotle combination and like to serve it with accompaniments that continue the southwestern theme, such as sweet potatoes or squash and seasoned black beans.

Tip

To purée gingerroot: Use a fine, sharp-toothed grater, such as those made by Microplane®.

1	boneless pork double-loin roast, about 3 lbs (1.5 kg), trimmed and tied	1
2 tsp	grated orange zest	10 mL
2/3 cup	freshly squeezed orange juice	150 mL
1/2 tsp	grated lime zest	2 mL
2 tbsp	freshly squeezed lime juice	25 mL
1 tbsp	chili powder	15 mL
2	cloves garlic, minced	2
1 tsp	cracked black peppercorns	5 mL

Apricot Chipotle Stuffing

1 cup	chopped dried apricots	250 mL
2	cloves garlic, minced	2
2	chipotle peppers in adobo sauce	2
1/4 cup	cilantro leaves	50 mL
1 tsp	puréed gingerroot (see Tip, left)	5 mL

1. Cut the string holding the roast together and separate into 2 pieces. On a cutting board, using the flat side of a cleaver, pound each half to flatten it a bit. Set aside.

2. In a long shallow dish large enough to accommodate the pork or in a resealable plastic bag, combine orange zest and juice, lime zest and juice, chili powder, garlic and peppercorns. Add pork and turn to thoroughly coat the meat. Cover and refrigerate for at least 6 hours or overnight, turning several times.

3. *Apricot Chipotle Stuffing:* In a food processor, combine apricots, garlic, chipotle peppers, cilantro leaves and gingerroot. Pulse several times until the mixture is blended but apricots are still a bit chunky.

4. Remove pork from marinade and place on a cutting board, flat side up. Discard marinade. Spread flat side of each pork half with the apricot mixture. Press the 2 halves together and, beginning in the middle, retie the roast securely following the butcher's indentations. Also tie once end to end.

5. Load meat onto the spit rods, ensuring it is evenly balanced. Roast until an instant-read thermometer inserted into the thickest part of the meat registers 160°F (71°C), about 1 hour and 20 minutes (depending upon the diameter of your roast). Let rest for 5 minutes before carving.

Chili-Rubbed Pork Chops

SERVES 4

Nothing could be simpler than these tasty chops, which have a delightful southwestern flavor. They are delicious served alongside a pot of steaming baked beans, or, for a complete change of pace, try serving them with Marinated Roasted Peppers (see recipe, page 156).

Tips

If you don't have ancho or New Mexico chili powder, use an additional teaspoon (5 mL) blended chili powder instead.

For a more evenly browned result, use butterflied pork loin pork chops and spear them on the spit rods horizontally instead of roasting the meat in the basket. Cook them for the same amount of time or, if your oven offers this option, cook them in the B position (which cooks food closer to the heat source) until an instant-read thermometer inserted into the thickest part of the meat registers 160°F (71°C), about 20 minutes. Just be sure to double-check that no meat is coming in contact with any part of the oven when cooking this close to the heat.

Do not use "seasoned" pork in recipes that call for brining (see Tips, page 108).

Brine

2 tbsp	kosher salt	25 mL
2	cloves garlic, chopped	2
2	dried red chili peppers, crumbled	2
2	bay leaves, crumbled	2
2 tsp	granulated sugar	10 mL
1 cup	boiling water	250 mL
4 cups	cold water (approx.)	1 L
	Ice cubes	
4	bone-in pork loin chops, about 1 inch (2.5 cm) thick	4

Rub

2 tsp	chili powder	10 mL
1 tsp	ancho or New Mexico chili powder (see Tips, left)	5 mL
½ tsp	toasted cumin seeds, ground (see Tips, page 120)	2 mL
¼ tsp	freshly ground black pepper	1 mL
1 tbsp	walnut or olive oil	15 mL

1. *Brine:* In a non-reactive bowl large enough to easily accommodate the pork and brine, combine salt, garlic, chili peppers, bay leaves, sugar and boiling water. Stir until the salt is thoroughly dissolved. Add cold water and enough ice cubes to cool the solution to room temperature. Add pork chops and additional water, if necessary, to cover. Cover and refrigerate for at least 2 hours or for up to 6 hours.

2. *Rub:* In a small bowl, combine chili powders, cumin and pepper. Remove pork from brine. Discard brine. Rinse chops under cold running water and pat dry with paper towel. Spread rub over both sides of chops. Brush with oil. Place in rotisserie basket, close lid tightly and load onto the spit rod assembly. Roast until an instant-read thermometer inserted into the thickest part of the meat registers 160°F (71°C), about 30 minutes.

Chinese-Style Pork Chops

SERVES 4

*Here's a great way to
bump up the status of the
everyday pork chop. Brine
it to add juiciness, then
marinate briefly in Chinese
seasonings. After it is
roasted, slice it thinly and
serve over hot Chinese
Noodles, accompanied by
steamed spinach sprinkled
with toasted sesame seeds.*

Tips

For more even roasting and
a browner result, cook the
chops directly on the spit
rods. Spear the chops
horizontally so they are
evenly balanced. Roast for
the same amount of time.
Or if you have the speed
basket accessory and the
chops will fit, cook them
in the B position for about
20 minutes.

Do not use "seasoned" pork
in recipes that call for brining.
It has already been injected
with a brine containing salt
and sodium phosphate in a
water solution, so the product
is not recommended for
further brining since the
meat's cells are already
saturated with the solution.

Brine

1/4 cup	kosher salt	50 mL
1 cup	boiling water	250 mL
4 cups	cold water (approx.)	1 L
	Ice cubes	
2	butterflied pork loin chops, about 1 inch (2.5 cm) thick	2

Marinade

2 tbsp	hoisin sauce	25 mL
2 tbsp	soy sauce	25 mL
2 tbsp	liquid honey	25 mL
1 tbsp	rice vinegar	15 mL
1/4 tsp	ground cinnamon	1 mL
1/4 tsp	cayenne pepper	1 mL
	Chinese Noodles (see recipe, page 109)	

1. *Brine:* In a non-reactive bowl large enough to accommodate the pork and brine, combine salt and boiling water. Stir until the salt is thoroughly dissolved. Add cold water and enough ice cubes to cool the solution to room temperature. Add pork chops. Add additional water, if necessary, to cover. Cover and refrigerate for at least 2 hours or for up to 6 hours. Remove chops from brine. Discard brine. Rinse chops under cold running water and pat dry with paper towel.

2. *Marinade:* In a bowl, combine hoisin sauce, soy sauce, honey, vinegar, cinnamon and cayenne. Place pork in a shallow dish large enough to accommodate it in a single layer and pour the sauce over meat, turning to ensure all parts are covered. Cover and let stand at room temperature for 30 minutes.

3. Remove pork from marinade. Discard marinade. Place chops in rotisserie basket, close lid tightly and load onto the spit rod assembly. Roast until an instant-read thermometer inserted into the thickest part of the meat registers 160°F (71°C), about 30 minutes. Let rest for 5 minutes. Slice thinly and serve with Chinese Noodles.

Chinese Noodles

1. Cook 8 oz (250 g) dried Chinese egg noodles according to package directions. Drain and rinse under cold running water. Heat 1 tbsp (15 mL) vegetable oil in a skillet or wok over medium heat and sauté 1 tbsp (15 mL) minced garlic and 1 tsp (5 mL) minced gingerroot for 1 minute. Add 6 thinly sliced green onions (white part only) and 2 tbsp (25 mL) each oyster and soy sauces and stir well. Add cooked noodles and toss to combine. Transfer to a warm platter and drizzle with 1 tsp (5 mL) toasted sesame oil. Sprinkle with toasted sesame seeds, to taste, if desired.

Pork Chops
with Romesco Sauce

SERVES 4

Romesco sauce is Spanish in origin and is traditionally served with poultry or fish. It is particularly good with swordfish. Perhaps not surprisingly, it's delicious with pork as well and is a great way of transforming pork chops into an epicurean delight. I like to serve this with whole wheat pasta tossed in a little extra virgin olive oil, as well as a bowl of steaming Swiss chard or collard greens.

Tips

If you don't have a fresh hot red pepper, use 2 dried ones instead. Sauté them for 1 minute in the hot oil before adding the bread to the pan. Remove them from the tomato mixture and discard before transferring the sauce to the food processor.

If you prefer, use 4 bone-in chops and roast them in the rotisserie basket. Or if your machine has a B position, you can roast the chops on the spit rods, closer to the heat element, for about 20 minutes.

Romesco Sauce

¾ cup	extra virgin olive oil, divided	175 mL
1	slice country-style bread, about 1 inch (2.5 cm) thick, crusts removed	1
4	cloves garlic, minced	4
1	fresh red chili pepper (see Tips, left)	1
1 cup	drained chopped tomatoes	250 mL
1	roasted red bell pepper	1
½ cup	blanched almonds or pine nuts, toasted	125 mL
2 tbsp	red wine vinegar	25 mL
	Salt and freshly ground black pepper	

Brine

¼ cup	kosher salt	50 mL
1 cup	boiling water	250 mL
4 cups	cold water (approx.)	1 L
	Ice cubes	
2	large butterflied pork loin pork chops, about 1 inch (2.5 cm) thick	2
2 tsp	paprika	10 mL
1 tsp	cumin seeds, toasted and ground (see Tips, page 120)	5 mL
1 tsp	coarse sea salt, crushed (see Tips, right)	5 mL
Pinch	cayenne pepper	Pinch
1 tbsp	olive oil	15 mL

1. *Romesco Sauce:* In a skillet, heat 2 tbsp (25 mL) olive oil over medium heat. Add bread and fry, turning once, until both sides are golden, about 5 minutes. Transfer to a food processor.

To crush coarse sea salt: Use a mortar and a pestle, or place the salt between 2 sheets of waxed paper and crush with a rolling pin or the bottom of a measuring cup. The salt should retain its chunky texture but be fine enough to rub evenly over the meat.

Do not use "seasoned" pork in recipes that call for brining. It has already been injected with a brine containing salt and sodium phosphate in a water solution, so the product is not recommended for further brining since the meat's cells are already saturated with the solution.

2. Return skillet to element. Add garlic and chili pepper and cook, stirring, for 1 minute. Add tomatoes and bell pepper and bring to a boil. Transfer to food processor. Add almonds and vinegar and process until smooth. With motor running, add remaining olive oil in a steady stream through feed tube, processing until smooth. Taste and adjust seasoning. Transfer to a sauceboat. Cover and refrigerate for at least 4 hours or for up to 2 days to allow the flavors to develop.

3. *Brine:* In a non-reactive bowl large enough to easily accommodate the pork and brine, combine salt and boiling water. Stir until the salt is thoroughly dissolved. Add cold water and enough ice cubes to cool the solution to room temperature. Add pork chops. Add additional water, if necessary, to cover. Cover and refrigerate for at least 2 hours or for up to 6 hours. Remove chops from brine. Discard brine. Rinse chops under cold running water and pat dry with paper towel.

4. In a small bowl, combine paprika, cumin, salt and cayenne. Rub spice mixture into both sides of meat. Brush with olive oil. Thread chops onto the spit rods horizontally so they are evenly balanced, leaving space between to allow the heat to circulate. Roast until an instant-read thermometer inserted into the thickest part of the chop registers 160°F (71°C), about 30 minutes. Serve each guest half a chop topped with a dollop of Romesco Sauce and pass the remainder at the table.

Cider-Brined Pork Chops with Horseradish Glaze

SERVES 4

Here's a delightfully different way of brining pork. This is great with a steaming pot of baked beans and warm bread.

Tips

When glazing chops, I like to roast the meat directly on the spit rods in the B position because the close proximity to the heating element facilitates browning. If you prefer, you can roast the chops in the rotisserie basket (brush the chops with the glaze after removing them from the brine, rinsing and patting dry) for about 30 minutes. If you are roasting the chops on the spit rods in the A position, rinse and pat them dry after removing them from the brine, but do not brush them with the glaze until they have roasted for 10 minutes. Then stop the machine and brush them with the glaze. Roast for 10 minutes, then repeat. Roast until an instant-read thermometer inserted into the thickest part of the meat registers 160°F (71°C).

Do not use "seasoned" pork in recipes that call for brining (see Tips, page 108).

Brine

2 cups	apple cider or juice (approx.)	500 mL
1 tbsp	apple cider vinegar	15 mL
3 tbsp	kosher salt	45 mL
2	cloves garlic, minced	2
2	butterflied pork loin pork chops, about 1 inch (2.5 cm) thick	2

Horseradish Glaze

½ cup	apple jelly	125 mL
2 tbsp	prepared horseradish	25 mL

1. *Brine:* In a bowl large enough to easily accommodate the pork chops and brine, combine apple cider, vinegar, salt and garlic. Stir until salt is dissolved. Add pork and additional cider, if necessary, to cover. Cover and refrigerate for at least 4 hours or for up to 6 hours.

2. *Horseradish Glaze:* In a small bowl, combine apple jelly and horseradish. Set aside.

3. Remove chops from brine. Discard brine. Rinse chops under cold running water and pat dry with paper towel. Thread chops onto the spit rods horizontally so they are evenly balanced, leaving space between to allow the heat to circulate. Brush thoroughly with glaze. Roast in the B position, checking to make sure no food is coming in contact with the heating element (see Tip, left). Roast, stopping the machine twice to baste the chops with additional glaze, until an instant-read thermometer inserted into the thickest part of the meat registers 160°F (71°C), about 20 minutes.

4. Remove the chops from the spit rods. Let rest for 5 minutes and serve. Pass Horseradish Glaze alongside.

Pork and Zucchini Brochettes

SERVES 4 TO 6

This makes a great weekday dinner. I like to serve the vegetable and meat chunks over Easy Pine Nut Pilaf (see recipe, page 99). A tossed green salad completes the meal.

Tips

These days, there are many sweet fruit vinegars on the market that would work well in this recipe. Use whatever appeals to you.

To purée garlic: Use a fine, sharp-toothed grater, such as those made by Microplane®.

2	onions, minced	2
1/2 cup	olive oil	125 mL
1/4 cup	sweet plum vinegar (see Tips, left)	50 mL
2 tbsp	puréed garlic, 6 to 8 cloves (see Tips, left)	25 mL
1/2 tsp	dried thyme leaves	2 mL
2	pork tenderloins, each about 12 oz (375 g), cut into 1-inch (2.5 cm) thick slices	2
4	small zucchini, cut into 1-inch (2.5 cm) slices	4
2 tsp	salt	10 mL
2 tbsp	olive oil	25 mL
2 tbsp	fresh thyme leaves or finely chopped parsley, optional	25 mL

1. In a resealable plastic bag or a shallow dish, combine onions, 1/2 cup (125 mL) olive oil, vinegar, garlic and thyme. Add pork and toss to coat. Cover and refrigerate overnight.

2. In a colander, combine zucchini and salt. Let stand over a bowl in sink to sweat for 30 minutes. Rinse and pat dry with paper towel. Toss with 2 tbsp (25 mL) olive oil.

3. Remove pork from marinade. Discard marinade. Pat pork dry with paper towel and thread onto kabob rods, alternating with zucchini, leaving space between to allow the heat to circulate. Load onto the gear wheels with spring ends on the right, or according to the manufacturer's instructions for rotation. Roast until just a hint of pink remains in the center of the pork, about 30 minutes. Remove from rods. Sprinkle with thyme, if using, and serve.

Spanish-Style Pork Kabobs

These tasty kabobs are the epitome of casual dining. Serve them with Marinated Roasted Peppers (see recipe, page 156) and wrap them in a pita for a change.

Tips

To crush coarse sea salt: Use a mortar and a pestle, or place the salt between 2 sheets of waxed paper and crush with a rolling pin or the bottom of a measuring cup. The salt should retain its chunky texture but be fine enough to rub evenly over the meat.

To purée garlic: Use a fine, sharp-toothed grater, such as those made by Microplane®.

1 tbsp	coarse sea salt, crushed (see Tips, left), or 1 tsp (5 mL) table salt	15 mL
¼ cup	finely chopped parsley	50 mL
2 tbsp	puréed garlic, 6 to 8 cloves (see Tips, left)	25 mL
2 tbsp	olive oil	25 mL
1 tbsp	paprika	15 mL
2 tsp	red wine vinegar	10 mL
2 tsp	cracked black peppercorns	10 mL
2	pork tenderloins, each about 12 oz (375 g), cut into 1-inch (2.5 cm) thick slices	2

1. In a small bowl, combine sea salt, parsley, garlic, olive oil, paprika, vinegar and peppercorns. Pat pork dry with paper towel and rub spice mixture into pork. Cover and refrigerate for at least 6 hours or overnight.

2. Remove pork from marinade. Discard marinade. Pat pork dry with paper towel and thread onto the kabob rods, leaving space between to allow the heat to circulate. Load onto the gear wheels with spring ends on the right, or according to the manufacturer's instructions for rotation. Roast until just a hint of pink remains in the center of the meat, about 30 minutes. Remove from rods and serve.

Rotisserie Ribs

Ribs taste great roasted on the rotisserie, and they are very easy to do. After being brined or preboiled, they are mounted on the spit rods, using the kabob rods to hold them in place (see diagrams, page 86). Whether you choose to brine or preboil ribs is a matter of choice. I prefer the texture of the meat when brined, but some people feel they are more tender if preboiled. All the recipes contain instructions for either method, so the choice is yours.

Tips

After the ribs are brined or preboiled, you can use one of the following recipes, or you can simply brush them with your favorite barbecue sauce and roast for about 30 minutes, until they are crisp and browned.

Do not use "seasoned" pork in recipes that call for brining. It has already been injected with a brine containing salt and sodium phosphate in a water solution. The product is not recommended for further brining since the meat's cells are already saturated with the solution.

All-Purpose Brine for Ribs

Brine

1/2 cup	kosher salt	125 mL
2	cloves garlic, crushed	2
2	dried hot peppers, crumbled	2
2	bay leaves, crumbled	2
2 cups	boiling water	500 mL
8 cups	cold water (approx.)	2 L
	Ice cubes	
2	racks pork baby back ribs, about 4 lbs (2 kg)	2

1. *Brine:* In a bowl or a stockpot large enough to easily accommodate the ribs and brine, combine salt, garlic, hot peppers and bay leaves. Cover with boiling water and stir until the salt dissolves. Stir in cold water and enough ice cubes to cool the solution to room temperature. Add ribs and additional cold water, if necessary, to ensure the meat is completely submerged in the brine. Cover and refrigerate for at least 4 hours or overnight.

2. Remove ribs from brine. Discard brine. Rinse ribs well under cold running water and pat dry with paper towel. Ribs are now ready for use in your recipe.

Parboiling Ribs

12 cups	water	3 L
2	cloves garlic, sliced	2
1 tsp	table salt	5 mL
10	whole black peppercorns	10
2	racks pork baby back ribs, about 4 lbs (2 kg)	2

1. In a stockpot over medium heat, bring water to a boil. Add garlic, salt, peppercorns and ribs. Return to a boil. Reduce heat to low. Cover and simmer for 15 minutes. Remove ribs from the pot. Pat dry with paper towel and proceed with recipe. If you're not roasting the ribs immediately, let cool and cover them tightly. Refrigerate until you're ready to use, up to 1 day.

Ribs in Adobo

This is a Spanish approach to roasting ribs. The sauce, although simple, is a very tasty combination of flavors that complement the pork.

Tips

To crush coarse sea salt: Use a mortar and a pestle, or place the salt between 2 sheets of waxed paper and crush with a rolling pin or the bottom of a measuring cup. The salt should retain its chunky texture but be fine enough to rub evenly over the meat.

For typical instructions for cooking ribs, see page 86.

2	racks pork baby back ribs, about 4 lbs (2 kg)	2
1 tbsp	olive oil	15 mL
1 tbsp	white wine vinegar	15 mL
1 tbsp	dried oregano leaves	15 mL
1 tbsp	paprika	15 mL
1 tsp	coarse sea salt, crushed (see Tips, left), or ½ tsp (2 mL) table salt	5 mL
½ tsp	cracked black peppercorns	2 mL
¼ tsp	cayenne pepper	1 mL

1. Brine or parboil ribs (see instructions, page 115).

2. In a small bowl, combine olive oil, vinegar, oregano, paprika, salt, peppercorns and cayenne. Rub into the meaty side of the ribs. Cover and refrigerate for at least 4 hours or overnight.

3. When ready to roast, place the gear wheel apparatus in the rest area position if your model has this feature, or follow the manufacturer's instructions for cooking ribs. Place 3 kabob rods in the holes around the wheel, with spring ends on the left, or according to the manufacturer's instructions for stability. Thread another kabob rod through the top end of the meat, just behind the first bone, and a second kabob rod through the rib at the bottom end of the meat. Repeat threading, using the same kabob rods to thread the second rack of ribs, so they are side by side on the rods. Insert the top rod into the gear wheels with the spring ends on the left, wrap the ribs around the 4 kabob rods already in place and insert the bottom rod into the gear wheels, with spring ends on the left.

4. Roast until the ribs are nicely browned, about 30 minutes. Remove ribs from the rotisserie and cut into individual pieces and serve.

Hoisin-Glazed Ribs

Tips

To purée garlic and gingerroot: Use a fine, sharp-toothed grater, such as those made by Microplane®.

For typical instructions for cooking ribs, see page 86.

2	racks pork baby back ribs, about 4 lbs (2 kg)	2
½ cup	hoisin sauce	125 mL
1 tbsp	liquid honey	15 mL
2 tsp	Asian chili sauce, such as sambal oelek	10 mL
1 tsp	puréed garlic	5 mL
1 tsp	puréed gingerroot	5 mL
1 tsp	cracked black peppercorns	5 mL
1 tsp	sesame oil	5 mL
2 tbsp	toasted sesame seeds	25 mL

1. Brine or parboil ribs (see instructions, page 115).

2. In a bowl, combine hoisin sauce, honey, chili sauce, garlic, gingerroot, peppercorns and sesame oil. Stir well.

3. Set aside half of the glaze. Brush ribs with remaining glaze.

4. Place the gear wheel apparatus in the rest area position if your model has this feature, or follow the manufacturer's instructions for cooking ribs. Place 3 kabob rods in the holes around the wheel, with the spring ends on the left, or according to the manufacturer's instructions for stability. (Continue threading following instructions in Step 3, opposite.) Insert the top rod into the gear wheels, with the spring ends on the left, wrap the ribs around the 3 kabob rods already in place and insert the bottom rod into the gear wheels, with the spring ends on the left. Roast until ribs are nicely browned, about 30 minutes. Remove ribs from the rotisserie and cut into individual pieces.

5. In a large bowl, combine reserved sauce and ribs. Toss until thoroughly coated. Arrange on a platter. Sprinkle with sesame seeds and serve.

Variation

Spicy Chinese Ribs: In a small saucepan over medium heat, combine 2 tbsp (25 mL) liquid honey, 1 tbsp (15 mL) each Asian chili sauce, dark soy sauce and rice vinegar, ½ tsp (2 mL) puréed garlic and ¾ cup (175 mL) chicken stock. Bring to a boil. Add 1 tbsp (15 mL) cornstarch dissolved in 2 tbsp (25 mL) water and cook, stirring, until thickened. Proceed with Step 3.

Café au Chili Ribs

This is a recipe for a coffee-flavored barbecue sauce that I adapted from Mark Miller, the chef-anthropologist who pioneered southwestern cuisine. It has intriguing and quite addictive flavors and, in my mind at least, inspires cowgirl fantasies of campfire cooking.

Tips

I prefer the clean, crisp taste and enhanced mineral content of sea salt over refined table salt, which has a bitter, acrid taste. I always have plenty of sea salt on hand in my kitchen, but you can use tiny quantities of table salt in its place, if you prefer.

For typical instructions for cooking ribs, see page 86.

2	racks pork baby back ribs, about 4 lbs (2 kg)	2
Sauce		
3	dried ancho chili peppers, stems removed	3
1	dried chipotle pepper, stem removed, optional	1
1 tbsp	vegetable oil	15 mL
1	onion, chopped	1
4	cloves garlic, chopped	4
1 tsp	fine sea salt or table salt (see Tip, left)	5 mL
1 tsp	cracked black peppercorns	5 mL
2 tbsp	cider vinegar	25 mL
1	can (28 oz/796 mL) tomatoes, drained and coarsely chopped	1
1 cup	strong brewed coffee	250 mL
¼ cup	fancy molasses	50 mL

1. Brine or parboil ribs (see instructions, page 115).

2. *Sauce:* In a dry skillet over medium heat, stir ancho peppers and chipotle pepper, if using, until they release their aroma, about 3 minutes. Transfer to a cutting board. Let cool and cut into quarters. Set aside.

3. Return skillet to element and heat vegetable oil over medium heat. Add onion and cook, stirring, until softened, about 3 minutes. Add garlic, salt and peppercorns and cook, stirring, for 1 minute. Add vinegar and cook, stirring, until it evaporates, about 2 minutes. Add tomatoes, coffee, molasses and reserved chilies, if using, and bring to a boil. Reduce heat to low and simmer until chilies are soft and sauce has thickened, about 20 minutes.

4. Transfer mixture to a food processor and process until smooth. Place a strainer over a large bowl and add puréed mixture. Using a wooden spoon, press the mixture through the strainer until all the liquid and most of the solids have been extracted.

5. Pour off $\frac{1}{2}$ cup (125 mL) of the sauce to use for basting and distribute the remainder among 4 individual serving bowls. Brush the ribs with the basting sauce.

6. Place the gear wheel apparatus in the rest area position if your model has this feature, or follow the manufacturer's instructions for cooking ribs. Place 4 kabob rods in the holes around the wheel, with the spring ends on the left, or according to the manufacturer's instructions for stability. Thread another kabob rod through the top end of the meat, just behind the first bone, and a second kabob rod through the rib at the bottom end of the meat. Repeat threading, using the same kabob rods to thread the second rack of ribs, so they are side by side on the rods. Insert the top rod into the gear wheels, with the spring end on the left, wrap the ribs around the 4 kabob rods already in place and insert the bottom rod into the gear wheels, with the spring end on the left.

7. Roast for 30 minutes, stopping the machine twice to baste the ribs. Let ribs rest for 5 minutes. Remove ribs from the rotisserie and cut into individual pieces and serve, giving each diner a bowl of sauce for dipping.

Southwestern-Style Ribs

SERVES 4

A spicy rub with flavors of the Old West; serve these ribs with a steaming pot of baked beans to continue the frontier theme.

Tips

If you don't have sherry vinegar for the variation, use balsamic, apple cider vinegar or white vinegar in this recipe.

To toast cumin seeds: Heat the seeds in a dry skillet over medium heat, stirring frequently, until the spices release their aroma and just begin to brown, 3 to 4 minutes. Immediately transfer to a spice grinder or a mortar and grind. You can also grind the spices on a cutting board using the bottom of a wine bottle or measuring cup.

For typical instructions for cooking ribs, see page 86.

2	racks pork baby back ribs, about 4 lbs (2 kg)	2
1 tbsp	New Mexico chili powder	15 mL
1 tbsp	cumin seeds, toasted and ground	15 mL
1 tsp	dried oregano, preferably Mexican	5 mL
1/2 tsp	cracked black peppercorns	2 mL
1/4 tsp	cayenne pepper	1 mL
1 tbsp	olive oil	15 mL

1. Brine or parboil ribs (see instructions, page 115).

2. In a small bowl, combine chili powder, cumin, oregano, peppercorns and cayenne. Stir to blend.

3. Rub mixture into the meaty side of the ribs and brush with olive oil.

4. Place the gear wheel apparatus in the rest area position if your model has this feature, or follow the manufacturer's instructions for cooking ribs. Place 4 kabob rods in the holes around the wheel, with the spring ends on the left, or according to the manufacturer's instructions for stability. Thread another kabob rod through the top end of the meat, just behind the first bone, and a second kabob rod through the rib at the bottom end of the meat. Repeat threading, using the same kabob rods to thread the second rack of ribs, so they are side by side on the rods. Insert the top rod into the gear wheels, with the spring ends on the left, wrap the ribs around the 4 kabob rods already in place and insert the bottom rod into the gear wheels, with the spring end on the left. Roast until the meat is nicely browned, about 30 minutes. Remove ribs from the rotisserie and cut into individual pieces and serve.

Variation

Sherry-Glazed Ribs: In a small bowl, mix together 2 tbsp (25 mL) packed brown sugar and 1 tbsp (15 mL) sherry vinegar. Set aside. Arrange the ribs on the gear wheels as outlined in Step 4 and roast for 10 minutes. Brush the ribs with the glaze and continue roasting until ribs are crisp and nicely browned, about 20 minutes.

Fish and Seafood

The rotisserie oven is an easy way to cook fish and seafood. You don't need to add a lot of fat — a light brushing with olive oil is usually enough to do the trick. If you want to enhance the flavor, you can add rubs, marinades or glazes to suit your taste. Because it is so delicate, most fish cooks better in the rotisserie basket than directly on the spit rods. Fillets and steaks are done in no time — about 20 minutes. Shellfish, such as shrimp, scallops or rock lobster tails, cook beautifully on the kabob rods. In my experience, shrimp and lobster tails benefit from a brief brining before cooking, which makes them firm and juicy.

The simplest way to cook fish fillets or steaks is to pat them dry with paper towels, brush with a little olive oil and rub both sides with your favorite seasoning blend. Place in the rotisserie basket, close lid tightly and load onto the spit rod assembly. Cook until the fish flakes easily when pierced with a knife, about 20 minutes.

The following seasoning blends, which you're likely to have on hand, can be used to prepare delicious, no-fuss fish:

- sea salt or seasoned salt and freshly ground black pepper
- lemon pepper
- herbes de Provence
- dried Italian seasoning
- Cajun seasoning
- chili powder
- Old Bay seasoning
- berbere rub (for halibut or swordfish), see page 28
- your favorite spice blend

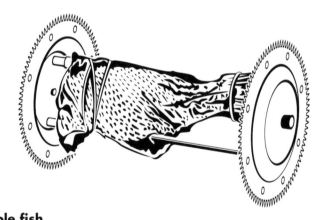

Whole fish

Threading whole fish, such as a large trout (see recipe, page 135), or any fish within the same weight range, onto the spit rods is a technique that produces great results. Using one of the spit rods as a long skewer, spear the trout up the backbone, working the rod in and out to secure it. Tie tightly with string on the right and left end of the fish to anchor it to the second spit rod. Trim any dangling twine. If your machine has a B position, use it; roasting the fish closer to the heat source produces a crispier result.

Salmon in Black Bean Sauce

SERVES 4

This convenient recipe takes advantage of prepared black bean sauce to produce great flavor with a minimum of effort. I like to serve this with plain white rice and baby bok choy stir-fried with ginger and garlic.

Black Bean Sauce

1 tsp	grated orange zest	5 mL
½ cup	freshly squeezed orange juice	125 mL
2 tbsp	black bean sauce with garlic	25 mL
1 tsp	cornstarch dissolved in 1 tbsp (15 mL) mirin or sweet sherry	5 mL
4	salmon steaks, 1 ½ to 2 lbs (750 g to 1 kg)	4
1 tbsp	olive oil	15 mL
2 tbsp	finely chopped green onion	25 mL

1. *Black Bean Sauce:* In a small saucepan over medium heat, combine orange zest and juice and black bean sauce. Bring to a boil and simmer for 1 minute. Add cornstarch mixture and cook, stirring, until thickened, about 30 seconds. Remove from heat and set aside.

2. Pat salmon dry with paper towel. Brush with olive oil. Place in rotisserie basket, close lid tightly and load onto the spit rod assembly. Cook until the fish flakes easily when pierced with a knife, about 20 minutes. Transfer to a warm platter. Pour reserved sauce over salmon. Sprinkle with green onion and serve.

> ## Variation
> *Scallops in Black Bean Sauce:* Substitute 1 lb (500 g) scallops for the salmon. Cook in rotisserie basket or on kabob rods, as you prefer. Large scallops will need to cook for about 20 minutes, smaller for about 15, until opaque and somewhat firm (but not overly firm or they will be chewy).

Salmon with Peperonata

SERVES 4 TO 6

*Peperonata, a flavorful
Italian (or French, known
as* **piperade***) stew of peppers
and tomatoes, is a wonderful
dish to make in the late
summer, when these
vegetables are in season.
I often serve it with a plain
omelet, but it also makes a
delicious, if untraditional,
partner for salmon.*

Tips

I like to use tricolored
peppers in this recipe for
their visual appeal. If it is
more convenient, make the
sauce with red peppers only.
It will taste just as good.

Most salmon fillets are cut
from the tail and weigh a
maximum of about 1½ lbs
(750 g). If you're lucky
enough to have a
fishmonger who will cut
you a nice center piece,
you'll end up with one
that is closer to 2 lbs (1 kg).

Peperonata

1 tbsp	olive oil	15 mL
1	onion, finely chopped	1
4	cloves garlic, minced	4
1	red bell pepper, thinly sliced on the vertical	1
1	orange bell pepper, thinly sliced on the vertical	1
1	yellow bell pepper, thinly sliced on the vertical	1
2	tomatoes, finely chopped	2
1 tbsp	balsamic or red wine vinegar	15 mL
2 tbsp	finely chopped parsley	25 mL
	Salt and freshly ground black pepper	
1	salmon fillet, 1½ to 2 lbs (750 g to 1 kg)	1
1 tbsp	olive oil	15 mL

1. *Peperonata:* In a skillet, heat oil over medium heat. Add onion and cook, stirring, until softened, about 3 minutes. Add garlic and cook, stirring, for 1 minute. Add red, orange and yellow peppers and cook, stirring occasionally, until softened, about 20 minutes. Add tomatoes and cook, stirring, for 5 minutes. Remove from heat. Stir in vinegar and parsley. Season with salt and pepper, to taste. Set aside.

2. Pat salmon dry with paper towel. Brush with olive oil. Place in rotisserie basket, close lid tightly and load onto the spit rod assembly. Cook until the fish flakes easily when pierced with a knife, 20 to 25 minutes.

3. To serve, ladle the Peperonata onto a deep platter or individual serving plates and arrange the salmon on top.

Salmon with Spicy Tomato Olive Sauce

SERVES 4 TO 6

The robust flavors of this Mediterranean-inspired sauce provide a nice balance for the rich but mild-tasting salmon.

Tomato Olive Sauce

1 tbsp	olive oil	15 mL
1	onion, chopped	1
2	cloves garlic, minced	2
1	green bell pepper, diced	1
1	long red or green chili pepper, diced, optional	1
1 tsp	salt	5 mL
½ tsp	cracked black peppercorns	2 mL
½ cup	dry white wine	125 mL
1	can (28 oz/796 mL) tomatoes, including juice, coarsely chopped	1
12	sliced green pimento-stuffed olives	12
1	salmon fillet, 1½ to 2 lbs (750 g to 1 kg)	1
1 tbsp	olive oil	15 mL

1. *Tomato Olive Sauce:* In a skillet, heat oil over medium heat. Add onion and cook, stirring, until softened, about 3 minutes. Add garlic, bell pepper, chili pepper, if using, salt and peppercorns and cook, stirring, for 1 minute. Add wine and cook, stirring, until reduced by half. Stir in tomatoes with juice and bring to a boil. Reduce heat to low and simmer until sauce thickens, about 20 minutes. Stir in olives and cook until heated through, about 1 minute.

2. Meanwhile, pat salmon dry with paper towel. Brush with olive oil. Place in rotisserie basket, close lid tightly and load onto the spit rod assembly. Cook until the fish flakes easily when pierced with a knife, 20 to 25 minutes. Transfer to a warm deep platter and cover with Tomato Olive Sauce. Serve immediately.

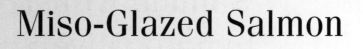

Miso-Glazed Salmon

SERVES 4 TO 6

Salmon and miso are a powerful combination, so this dish, although simple to make, is loaded with flavor. Miso, a fermented soybean paste, is available in well-stocked supermarkets or natural food stores. I like to serve this with stir-fried Chinese vegetables and steaming white rice.

Tip

Shaoxing wine is a Chinese rice wine often used in Chinese cooking. Although you can buy premium Shaoxing, suitable for drinking, in select liquor stores, many Asian markets carry a cooking-grade version. If you don't see it on the shelves, inquire. It's sometimes kept behind the counter.

¼ cup	soy sauce	50 mL
2 tbsp	Shaoxing wine or dry sherry (see Tip, left)	25 mL
2 tbsp	white miso paste	25 mL
1 tsp	puréed gingerroot	5 mL
1 tbsp	sesame oil	15 mL
1	long red or green chili pepper, minced, optional	1
1	salmon fillet, 1 ½ to 2 lbs (750 g to 1 kg)	1
2 tbsp	toasted sesame seeds, optional	25 mL

1. In a shallow dish large enough to accommodate the salmon in a single layer or in a resealable plastic bag, combine soy sauce, Shaoxing wine, miso, gingerroot, sesame oil and chili pepper, if using. Add salmon, turning several times to ensure it is well coated. Let stand at room temperature, skin side up, for 30 minutes.

2. Remove salmon from the marinade. Discard marinade. Place in rotisserie basket, close lid tightly and load onto the spit rod assembly. Cook until the fish flakes easily when pierced with a knife, 20 to 25 minutes. Transfer to a serving platter and sprinkle with sesame seeds, if using.

Warm Roasted Salmon Salad

SERVES 4

This gorgeous-looking composed salad makes a fabulous luncheon dish or a great light dinner on a warm summer night. All you need to add is a crisp white wine and wait for the compliments.

Tip

If you don't have white wine vinegar with tarragon, you can flavor this salad with fresh dill instead. Substitute 2 tbsp (25 mL) white wine or champagne vinegar. Add 2 tbsp (25 mL) finely chopped dill to the mixture along with the parsley.

1 lb	small new potatoes, skin on	500 g
1	shallot, minced	1
1 tsp	Dijon mustard	5 mL
2 tbsp	finely chopped parsley	25 mL
2 tbsp	white wine vinegar with tarragon (see Tip, left)	25 mL
7 tbsp	extra virgin olive oil, divided Salt and freshly ground black pepper	105 mL
2 cups	small peas, cooked and drained	500 mL
1	salmon fillet, about 12 oz (375 g)	1
4 cups	mixed salad greens	1 L
4	green onions, thinly sliced	4

1. In a large pot, cover potatoes with cold salted water and bring to a boil. Reduce heat and simmer until fork-tender, 15 to 20 minutes. Drain and let cool.

2. Meanwhile, in a bowl, whisk together shallot, mustard, parsley and vinegar until well blended. Gradually whisk in 6 tbsp (90 mL) olive oil until blended. Season with salt and pepper, to taste. Add peas, toss well and set aside.

3. Pat salmon dry with paper towel. Brush with remaining olive oil. Place in rotisserie basket, close lid tightly and load onto the spit rod assembly. Cook until the fish flakes easily when pierced with a knife, about 20 minutes. Remove from basket and let rest for 5 minutes. Cut into bite-size pieces.

4. Cut potatoes into thin slices. Arrange salad greens over the bottom of a deep platter or shallow serving bowl. Lay potatoes over top and sprinkle with onions. Spread salmon evenly over top. Spoon pea mixture evenly over the salmon and serve.

Roasted Salmon with Avocado and Mixed Greens

SERVES 4

Here's another great salmon salad that is perfect for lunch or a light dinner. It takes advantage of avocado, one of my favorite foods, not only because it's delicious and nutrient-rich but also because it's so convenient. I love the hint of walnut in the vinaigrette, but the dish is still delicious without it.

Tip

If you don't have walnut oil, use an extra tablespoon (15 mL) extra virgin olive oil instead.

1 tbsp	freshly squeezed lemon juice	15 mL
1/4 tsp	salt	1 mL
3 tbsp	olive oil	45 mL
1	salmon fillet, about 12 oz (375 g)	1

Vinaigrette

2 tbsp	white wine vinegar	25 mL
1/2 tsp	salt	2 mL
1/4 cup	extra virgin olive oil	50 mL
1 tbsp	walnut oil (see Tip, left)	15 mL
	Freshly ground black pepper	
6 cups	mixed salad greens	1.5 L
1	avocado	1
4	green onions, white part only, thinly sliced	4

1. In a bowl, combine lemon juice and salt, stirring until salt dissolves. Gradually whisk in olive oil. Place salmon in a shallow dish and cover with mixture. Turn to coat. Let stand at room temperature for 15 minutes.

2. Place salmon in rotisserie basket, close lid tightly and load onto the spit rod assembly. Cook until the fish flakes easily when pierced with a knife, about 20 minutes. Remove from basket and let rest for 5 minutes. Cut into bite-size pieces.

3. *Vinaigrette:* In a bowl, combine vinegar and salt, stirring until salt dissolves. Gradually whisk in olive oil and walnut oil until blended. Season with pepper, to taste. Set aside.

4. Arrange salad greens over the bottom of a deep platter or shallow serving bowl. Slice avocado and arrange it evenly over the greens. Sprinkle with onions. Spread salmon evenly over the top of the onions and drizzle with reserved vinaigrette, to taste. Serve immediately.

Rack of Baby Lamb with Green Sauce (page 98)

Overleaf: Assorted Roasted Vegetables (see Vegetables, page 145)

Halibut with Cilantro Chili Butter

SERVES 4 TO 6

Halibut is one of my favorite fish. A large fish with glistening white fillets, it's mildly flavored and responds well to a wide variety of seasonings. Here, it's paired with the Latin American combination of chilies, cilantro and lime.

Tips

If you are using unsalted butter, you may want to add a bit of salt, to taste, to the Cilantro Chili Butter.

Thick fillets of any firm white fish, such as red snapper, haddock or grouper, also work well in this recipe. I use an especially thick halibut fillet. If you're using smaller pieces of halibut or fillets of a different but smaller fish, such as snapper, reduce the cooking time by 5 to 10 minutes, depending upon the size.

1	halibut fillet, about 2 lbs (1 kg)	1
½ cup	olive oil	125 mL
¼ cup	freshly squeezed lime juice	50 mL
2	dried red chilies, crumbled	2
½ tsp	salt	2 mL

Cilantro Chili Butter

½ cup	butter, at room temperature	125 mL
1 or 2	long red or green chili or jalapeño peppers, finely chopped	1 or 2
¼ cup	finely chopped cilantro leaves	50 mL
1	green onion, white part only, finely chopped	1
2 tsp	finely grated lime zest	10 mL
1 tbsp	freshly squeezed lime juice (approx.)	15 mL
	Salt, optional (see Tips, left)	

1. Rinse halibut thoroughly under cold running water and pat dry with paper towel. In a dish large enough to accommodate the fish in a single layer or in a resealable plastic bag, combine olive oil, lime juice, chilies and salt. Add fish and turn to coat thoroughly. Let stand at room temperature for 30 minutes.

2. *Cilantro Chili Butter:* Meanwhile, in a mini-chopper or a bowl using a wooden spoon, combine butter, chili pepper, cilantro, green onion, lime zest and juice and salt, to taste, if using. Add additional lime juice, if desired. Spoon into a dish. Cover and refrigerate until ready to use, for up to 2 days.

3. Remove halibut from the marinade. Discard marinade. Place in rotisserie basket, close lid tightly and load onto the spit rod assembly. Cook until the fish flakes easily when pierced with a knife, about 30 minutes. Transfer to a warm platter. Dot with 2 or 3 pats of Cilantro Chili Butter and serve additional butter alongside.

> ### Variation
> *Halibut in Lime Cilantro Vinaigrette:* In a bowl, combine ¼ cup (50 mL) freshly squeezed lime juice, 2 tbsp (25 mL) soy sauce, 1 tbsp finely chopped cilantro, 1 tsp (5 mL) puréed gingerroot and 1 tbsp (15 mL) extra virgin olive oil. Drizzle over cooked fish instead of using the butter.

Chili-Roasted Loin of Pork with Apricot Chipotle Stuffing (page 106)

Italian-Style Swordfish

SERVES 4 TO 6

This is a classic Italian way of preparing swordfish. I've found that swordfish can easily dry out when cooked on the grill, but this isn't a problem on the rotisserie, which produces succulent results. If you're concerned about swordfish being over-fished, ask your fishmonger for harpooned rather than net-caught fish, which is more sustainable.

1 cup	extra virgin olive oil	250 mL
1 tbsp	grated lemon zest	15 mL
1 cup	freshly squeezed lemon juice	250 mL
1 cup	loosely packed parsley leaves	250 mL
1/2 cup	hot water	125 mL
1 tbsp	minced garlic	15 mL
1 tsp	dried oregano leaves	5 mL
1 tsp	coarse sea salt or 1/2 tsp (2 mL) table salt	5 mL
2	dried red chili peppers	2
1	swordfish steak, about 2 lbs (1 kg)	1
1 tbsp	drained capers	15 mL

1. In a blender or food processor, combine olive oil, lemon zest and juice, parsley, hot water, garlic, oregano and salt. Blend until parsley is finely chopped. Pour off 1 cup (250 mL) of the mixture, cover and refrigerate until the fish is ready. Add chili peppers to the remainder and blend for 30 seconds.

2. Rinse swordfish under cold running water and pat dry with paper towel. In a dish large enough to accommodate fish in a single layer or in a resealable plastic bag, combine swordfish and the mixture remaining in the blender. Let stand at room temperature for 30 minutes or in the refrigerator, covered, for up to 2 hours.

3. Remove swordfish from marinade. Discard marinade. Place in rotisserie basket, close lid tightly and load onto the spit rod assembly. Cook until the fish flakes easily when pierced with a knife, about 25 minutes. Transfer to a deep platter.

4. Add capers to refrigerated olive oil mixture. Stir well and pour over hot fish.

Swordfish with Anchovies and Olives

SERVES 4 TO 6

Swordfish is one of the few fish that can stand up to the powerful, but delectable, combination of anchovies and olives. This tangy sauce provides a perfect finish for the fish. I like to serve this with sliced tomatoes drizzled with extra virgin olive oil and a hint of good balsamic vinegar to complete the Mediterranean flavors.

Anchovy and Olive Sauce

2 cups	packed parsley leaves	500 mL
20	pitted black olives	20
2	anchovy fillets, chopped	2
2	cloves garlic, chopped	2
2 tbsp	freshly squeezed lemon juice	25 mL
1/4 cup	olive oil	50 mL
1	swordfish steak, about 2 lbs (1 kg)	1
1/2 cup	olive oil	125 mL
1/4 cup	freshly squeezed lemon juice	50 mL
2	dried red chili peppers, crushed	2
1/2 tsp	salt	2 mL
1/2 tsp	cracked black peppercorns	2 mL

1. *Anchovy and Olive Sauce:* In a food processor, combine parsley, olives, anchovies, garlic and lemon juice. Process until ingredients are combined. With motor running, gradually add olive oil through the feed tube, until the mixture is smooth and blended. Refrigerate for at least 1 hour to allow flavors to blend, or for up to 2 days.

2. Rinse swordfish under cold running water and pat dry with paper towel. In a shallow dish large enough to accommodate the fish in a single layer or in a resealable plastic bag, combine olive oil, lemon juice, chili peppers, salt and peppercorns. Add swordfish and coat with mixture. Let stand at room temperature for 30 minutes or in refrigerator, covered, for up to 2 hours.

3. Remove swordfish from the marinade. Discard marinade. Place in rotisserie basket, close lid tightly and load onto the spit rod assembly. Cook until the fish flakes easily when pierced with a knife, about 25 minutes. Serve immediately, with the Anchovy and Olive Sauce alongside.

Swordfish with Creamy Sun-Dried Tomato Pesto

SERVES 4 TO 6

The intense flavors of sun-dried tomatoes and tarragon are a perfect finish for swordfish. All you need to add is a tossed green salad and some chilled white wine.

Tips

If you don't have tarragon vinegar, substitute an equal quantity of white wine or champagne vinegar and increase the amount of chopped tarragon by 1 tsp (5 mL).

If you don't like the taste of tarragon, you can make this sauce using white wine or champagne vinegar instead of tarragon vinegar, substituting an equal quantity of fresh thyme, parsley leaves or finely snipped chives for the tarragon.

Sun-Dried Tomato Pesto

1 cup	chicken or vegetable stock	250 mL
1 cup	dry white wine	250 mL
1/4 cup	white wine vinegar with tarragon (see Tips, left)	50 mL
1/2 cup	drained oil-packed sun-dried tomatoes	125 mL
1 tbsp	chopped fresh tarragon leaves (see Tips, left)	15 mL
2 tbsp	whipping (35%) cream	25 mL
	Salt and freshly ground black pepper	
1	swordfish steak, about 2 lbs (1 kg)	1
1/2 cup	olive oil	125 mL
1/4 cup	freshly squeezed lemon juice	50 mL
2	dried red chili peppers, crushed	2
1/2 tsp	salt	2 mL
1/2 tsp	cracked black peppercorns	2 mL

1. *Sun-Dried Tomato Pesto:* In a saucepan over medium heat, combine stock, wine and vinegar. Bring to a boil and cook until reduced to 1 cup (250 mL), about 10 minutes.

2. In a food processor, combine tomatoes and reduced stock mixture. Process until smooth. Add tarragon and cream and pulse until blended. Season with salt and pepper, to taste. Set aside.

3. Rinse swordfish under cold running water and pat dry with paper towel. In a shallow dish large enough to accommodate the fish in a single layer or in a resealable plastic bag, combine olive oil, lemon juice, chili peppers, salt and peppercorns. Add swordfish and coat with mixture. Let stand at room temperature, covered, for 30 minutes or in refrigerator for up to 2 hours.

4. Remove swordfish from the marinade. Discard marinade. Place in rotisserie basket, close lid tightly and load onto the spit rod assembly. Cook until the fish flakes easily when pierced with a knife, about 25 minutes. Transfer to a warm platter. Serve the pesto on the side.

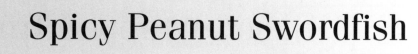

Spicy Peanut Swordfish

SERVES 4 TO 6

Spicy peanut sauce, an Asian treat, is traditionally served on noodles or as an accompaniment to satay. Here, it makes a tasty marinade for swordfish. Serve this with Chinese Noodles (see recipe, page 109) and stir-fried bok choy to complete the Asian theme.

Tip

To purée garlic and gingerroot: Use a fine, sharp-toothed grater, such as those made by Microplane®.

2 tbsp	creamy peanut butter	25 mL
2 tbsp	boiling water	25 mL
1 tbsp	grated lime zest	15 mL
½ cup	freshly squeezed lime juice	125 mL
2 tbsp	soy sauce	25 mL
2 tbsp	vegetable oil	25 mL
2 tbsp	sesame oil	25 mL
1 tbsp	puréed gingerroot	15 mL
1 tsp	puréed garlic	5 mL
1	long red or green chili pepper, minced, optional	1
1	swordfish steak, about 2 lbs (1 kg)	1

1. In a small bowl, combine peanut butter and boiling water. Stir until well blended. Add lime zest and juice, soy sauce, vegetable and sesame oils, gingerroot, garlic and chili pepper, if using. Set aside.

2. Rinse swordfish under cold running water and pat dry with paper towel. Place in a shallow dish large enough to accommodate fish in a single layer or in a resealable plastic bag and add the peanut butter mixture. Turn the swordfish to coat it thoroughly and let stand at room temperature for 30 minutes.

3. Remove swordfish from the marinade. Discard marinade. Place in rotisserie basket, close lid tightly and load onto the spit rod assembly. Cook until the fish flakes easily when pierced with a knife, about 25 minutes. Transfer to a warm platter and serve immediately.

Bacon-Wrapped Trout

SERVES 2 TO 4

Here's a simple way of cooking small-size trout that produces delicious results. Since most trout is farm raised and not as flavorful as the wild varieties, it benefits from the addition of savory bacon.

Tip

If your rotisserie has a speed basket, use it instead of the standard basket and cook in the B position to produce a crispier result. Reduce cooking time by about 5 minutes.

2	whole trout, cleaned and heads removed	2
	Sea salt	
	Freshly ground black pepper	
½	lemon, thinly sliced, then halved	½
	Parsley and/or chives	
1 tbsp	olive oil	15 mL
4 to 6	slices bacon, blanched for 1 minute in boiling water and drained	4 to 6

1. Rinse trout inside and out under cold running water and pat dry with paper towel. Season with salt and pepper, to taste. Place lemon slices in cavity then lay parsley sprigs and/or chives over the lemon. Brush the fish with olive oil. Wrap with bacon, securing with a small skewer, if necessary.

2. Place trout side by side in rotisserie basket, close lid tightly and load onto the spit rod assembly. Cook until the fish flakes easily when pierced with a knife, about 25 minutes. To serve, remove the bacon, fillet the fish and serve, accompanied by the cooked bacon, if desired.

> ### Variation
> *Pancetta-Wrapped Trout:* Substitute thinly sliced pancetta for the bacon. Do not blanch it before wrapping the fish.

Spit-Roasted Trout with Parsley Walnut Pesto

SERVES 4

It's a bit of work to thread a large trout onto the spit rods but, in my opinion, this technique produces great results. The fish is juicy and evenly cooked. If you prefer, use small trout and cook them in the rotisserie basket (see Bacon-Wrapped Trout, page 134, Step 2, for cooking instructions). I like to serve this with Pot-Roasted New Potatoes, in season (see recipe, page 103).

Tips

If you don't have walnut oil, use an additional tablespoon (15 mL) extra virgin olive oil instead.

If your rotisserie has a B position that cooks closer to the heat source, using it to cook the fish will produce a crispier result.

1	large trout, cleaned and head removed	1
2 tbsp	freshly squeezed lemon juice	25 mL
2 tbsp	olive oil	25 mL
1 tsp	coarse sea salt, crushed, or ½ tsp (2 mL) table salt	5 mL
	Freshly ground black pepper	

Parsley Walnut Pesto

2 cups	packed parsley leaves	500 mL
4	green onions, chopped	4
½ cup	walnuts	125 mL
¼ cup	freshly squeezed lemon juice	50 mL
¼ cup	extra virgin olive oil	50 mL
1 tbsp	walnut oil (see Tips, left)	15 mL
	Salt and freshly ground black pepper	

1. Rinse trout inside and out under cold running water and pat dry with paper towel. In a small bowl, combine lemon juice, olive oil, sea salt and pepper, to taste. Brush over cavity and rub into the skin of the fish.

2. Using one of the spit rods as a long skewer, spear the trout up the backbone, working the rod in and out to secure it. Tie tightly with string in 2 places to anchor it to the second spit rod (see diagram, page 122). Trim any dangling twine. Cook until the fish flakes easily when pierced with a knife, about 35 minutes.

3. *Parsley Walnut Pesto:* Meanwhile, in a food processor, combine parsley, green onions, walnuts and lemon juice and process until smooth. With motor running, gradually add olive oil then walnut oil through the feed tube, until mixture is smooth. Season with salt and pepper, to taste.

4. To serve: Fillet the fish and serve the pesto alongside.

Variation

Spit-Roasted Snapper with Parsley Walnut Pesto: Substitute a large red snapper, head removed and cleaned, for the trout.

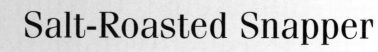

Salt-Roasted Snapper

SERVES 4

*This technique works well
for cooking small whole
fish, such as snapper and
trout, that have been gutted
and cleaned, with their
heads and tails removed.*

Tips

Crushing the sea salt lightly
ensures that the smaller
particles are more likely to
adhere to the skin of the fish
while the rotisserie turns.
Use a mortar and pestle or
the bottom of a wine bottle.
If you are using kosher salt,
you may be able to skip this
step, depending upon the
brand you use. Some are
finer than others. Judge
for yourself.

If your rotisserie has a speed
basket, use it instead of the
standard basket and cook
in the B position to produce
a crispier result. Reduce
cooking time by about
5 minutes.

2	whole red snappers, each about 12 oz (375 g), cleaned, heads and tails removed	2
2 tsp	dried oregano leaves, divided	10 mL
1 tbsp	freshly squeezed lemon juice	15 mL
2 tbsp	olive oil (approx.)	25 mL
½ cup	coarse sea or kosher salt, crushed if necessary (see Tips, left)	125 mL

1. Rinse snapper inside and out and pat dry with paper towel. Sprinkle each cavity with half the oregano and lemon juice.

2. Place the fish on their sides on a cutting board. Make 3 horizontal slashes in the skin of each. Sprinkle one side with ½ tsp (1 mL) of the remaining oregano and brush liberally with olive oil. Turn over and repeat on the other side.

3. Spread the sea salt over a plate and dredge the fish in the salt on both sides. Place snapper fillets side by side in the rotisserie basket, close lid tightly and load onto the spit rod assembly. Cook until the fish flakes easily when pierced with a knife, about 30 minutes.

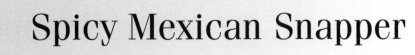

Spicy Mexican Snapper

SERVES 4 TO 6

This is a way of cooking snapper that I adapted from a recipe by Diana Kennedy, the doyenne of Mexican cooking. It produces a very flavorful result that can stand on its own as a main course, or it can be broken into pieces and used as filling for tortillas. I like to serve this with fresh tomato salsa or guacamole to continue the Mexican theme.

Tip

To purée garlic: Use a fine, sharp-toothed grater, such as those made by Microplane®.

1 tbsp	achiote seeds or paprika (see Tips, page 50)	15 mL
½ tsp	dried oregano leaves, preferably Mexican	2 mL
1 tsp	coarse sea salt or ½ tsp (2 mL) table salt	5 mL
1 tsp	puréed garlic	5 mL
2 tbsp	white wine vinegar	25 mL
Pinch	cayenne pepper	Pinch
2 lbs	red snapper fillets, skin on	1 kg
1 tbsp	olive oil	15 mL

1. In a spice grinder or in a mortar with a pestle, grind achiote seeds and oregano leaves to a fine powder. Add sea salt and pulse once or twice, or, if using a pestle, just until the salt is incorporated into the mixture. Transfer to a small bowl. Add garlic, vinegar and cayenne and blend well.

2. Rinse snapper under cold running water and pat dry with paper towel. Brush the skin side with olive oil and spread the spice mixture over the flesh side. Cover and refrigerate for 2 hours.

3. Place snapper fillets side by side in the rotisserie basket, close lid tightly and load onto the spit rod assembly. Cook until the fish flakes easily when pierced with a knife, about 20 minutes. Serve immediately.

Chili-Coated Snapper

SERVES 2

Nothing could be easier than this tasty coating, which turns simple fish fillets into a delicious meal. Double the recipe if desired and feel free to substitute any firm white fish for the snapper, if you prefer.

Tip

If you have a speed basket, by all means use it to cook the fish in the B position of your oven. Reduce the cooking time by about 5 minutes.

¼ cup	mayonnaise	50 mL
1 tbsp	Dijon mustard	15 mL
½ tsp	ancho chili powder	2 mL
¼ tsp	dried oregano leaves	1 mL
1 lb	snapper fillets, skin removed	500 g

1. In a small bowl, combine mayonnaise, mustard, chili powder and oregano. Set all but 1 tbsp (15 mL) of mixture aside.

2. Rinse snapper and pat dry. Brush both sides with 1 tbsp (15 mL) of the mixture.

3. Place snapper fillets side by side in the rotisserie basket, close lid tightly and load onto the spit rod assembly. Cook until the fish flakes easily when pierced with a knife, about 20 minutes. Serve immediately and pass remaining chili mayonnaise at the table.

Miso Butterfish

SERVES 4

This is a rich but delicious special-occasion dish based on one I ate at Ming Tsai's restaurant, Blue Ginger, in Wellesley, Massachusetts. I like to serve this with cold soba noodles tossed in an Asian vinaigrette.

½ cup	white miso paste	125 mL
¼ cup	mirin or sweet sherry	50 mL
¼ cup	vodka	50 mL
1 tbsp	olive oil	15 mL
1 tbsp	puréed gingerroot	15 mL
½ tsp	cracked black peppercorns	2 mL
1 ½ lbs	black cod or butterfish fillets, skin removed	750 g

1. In a shallow dish large enough to hold the fish in a single layer or in a resealable plastic bag, combine miso, mirin, vodka, olive oil, gingerroot and peppercorns. Mix well. Add butterfish and turn to coat thoroughly with the mixture. Cover and refrigerate overnight.

2. Remove butterfish from the marinade. Discard marinade. Pat dry with paper towel. Place fish fillets side by side in the rotisserie basket, close lid tightly and load onto the spit rod assembly. Cook until the fish flakes easily when pierced with a knife, about 25 minutes.

Bacon-Wrapped Scallops

SERVES 4 TO 8

Large scallops cook very well on the kabob rods, and they need very little done to them. I often buy mine from my fishmonger already wrapped in bacon, but it's easy to wrap them yourself, securing the bacon with a toothpick. Serve these as a light main course, or as a hot appetizer or party canapé.

Tips

This may seem like a lot of bacon for this quantity of scallops, but there will be a bit of waste. It's important to have enough bacon to ensure that the sides of each scallop are completely covered. Test-wrap each scallop, then trim the bacon to fit. Save the leftover pieces, cook them to a crisp and use as a garnish for vegetables or salads.

To add a pleasant hint of flavor, brush the scallops with a flavored oil, such as chili, lemon or oregano, instead of plain olive oil.

1 lb	large sea scallops	500 g
1 tbsp	olive oil	15 mL
8 oz	thinly sliced bacon	250 g
	Freshly ground black pepper	

1. Rinse scallops and pat dry with paper towel. Brush the tops and bottoms of the scallops with olive oil. Wrap a slice of bacon around the side of 1 scallop, to completely enclose it, then trim so it overlaps just slightly (see Tips, left). Secure with a toothpick. Repeat until all the scallops are wrapped.

2. Thread scallops onto the kabob rods, leaving enough space between them to allow the heat to circulate. Load rods onto the gear wheels with the spring ends on the right, or according to the manufacturer's instructions for rotation. Cook until the bacon is crisp and the scallops are cooked through, opaque and somewhat firm (but not overly firm or they will be chewy), about 20 minutes, depending upon the size. Remove from the kabob rods and season with pepper, to taste.

Variation

Pancetta-Wrapped Scallops: Substitute 8 oz (250 g) thinly sliced pancetta for the bacon. Cut each slice in half before wrapping.

Tiger Shrimp with Aïoli

SERVES 4

This is one of my favorite summer meals. Brining the shrimp firms them up and makes them succulent on the rotisserie, which cooks at a lower temperature than a barbecue, the traditional method of preparation.

Tips

The shrimp I use for this recipe are truly colossal, about 7 per pound. If you use smaller shrimp, adjust the cooking time accordingly.

Although plain vegetable oil does the job, you can add a whisper of flavor to the shrimp by brushing them with chili oil or a herb-infused oil such as lemon, garlic or oregano.

Raw eggs can be a vehicle for salmonella poisoning. I buy free-range organic eggs directly from a farmer on a weekly basis, and even then, there is no guarantee they won't carry the deadly bacteria. If you are at all concerned about your source, make Instant Aïoli (see Variations, page 141) using bottled mayonnaise.

2 lbs	tiger shrimp, shells on, about 14 shrimp (see Tips, left)	1 kg
Brine		
¼ cup	kosher salt or 2 tbsp (25 mL) table salt	50 mL
2	dried red chili peppers	2
4	cloves garlic, crushed	4
2 tsp	granulated sugar	10 mL
1 cup	boiling water	250 mL
4 cups	cold water (approx.)	1 L
2 tbsp	rice vinegar	25 mL
	Ice cubes	
¼ cup	vegetable oil (see Tips, left)	50 mL
Aïoli		
4	cloves garlic, coarsely chopped	4
2	egg yolks (see Tips, left)	2
2 tbsp	freshly squeezed lemon juice	25 mL
1 tsp	Dijon mustard	5 mL
1 tsp	salt	5 mL
½ tsp	freshly ground black pepper	2 mL
Pinch	cayenne, optional	Pinch
1 cup	olive oil	250 mL

1. Using a knife, slit the shrimp shells along the back, removing the vein but leaving the shells intact. Set aside.

2. *Brine:* In a large heatproof non-reactive bowl, combine salt, chilies, garlic, sugar and boiling water. Stir until salt and sugar are dissolved. Add cold water and vinegar and stir well. Add enough ice cubes to cool the mixture to room temperature.

3. Place shrimp in brining solution, adding additional cold water to cover, if necessary. Cover bowl and refrigerate for 30 minutes to 1 hour.

4. Remove shrimp from brine. Discard brine. Rinse shrimp under cold running water and pat dry with paper towel. Brush liberally with vegetable oil. Skewer onto the kabob rods, leaving space between to allow heat to circulate. Load rods onto the gear wheels with the spring ends on the right, or according to the manufacturer's instructions for rotation. Cook until the shells are very pink and the shrimp are cooked through, 10 to 15 minutes. Serve hot, in their shells, accompanied by Aïoli.

5. *Aïoli:* Meanwhile, in a food processor, combine garlic, egg yolks, lemon juice, mustard, salt, pepper and cayenne, if using. Process until mixture is smooth and well blended, about 1 minute. With the motor running, gradually add olive oil through the feed tube, pausing occasionally to ensure that the mixture is thickening and absorbing the oil. (If it appears to be too liquid, stop adding oil and continue processing until the mixture thickens.) Continue until all the oil is absorbed and the mixture is firm. Cover and chill until ready to use.

> ## Variations
>
> *Instant Aïoli:* Combine 1 cup (250 mL) mayonnaise with 2 tbsp (25 mL) minced garlic. Stir to blend.
>
> *Dill Aïoli:* Add 2 tbsp (25 mL) finely chopped dill to Aïoli or Instant Aïoli.
>
> *Spicy Aïoli:* Add 2 tbsp (25 mL) Asian chili sauce to Aïoli.

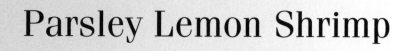

Parsley Lemon Shrimp

Shrimp kabobs make a great informal finger-food meal. People enjoy peeling their own shrimp and dipping them in a selection of sauces. Include finger bowls and an abundant supply of paper napkins as part of the fun. Vary the dipping sauces to suit your mood and feel free to use a prepared sauce or two, if you prefer.

Tips

Although they are more messy to eat, leaving the shells on the shrimp while they cook produces a more flavorful result.

For this recipe, I used extra-large shrimp, about 20 per pound. Depending upon the brand you purchase, shrimp this size may be labeled jumbo and even colossal — shrimp producers have a tendency to exaggerate the actual size of their shrimp.

2 lbs	large shrimp, shells on, about 40 shrimp (see Tips, left)	1 kg

Brine

1/4 cup	kosher salt	50 mL
2 cups	boiling water	500 mL
4 cups	cold water (approx.)	1 L
	Ice cubes	
	Olive oil	

Parsley Lemon Butter

1/2 cup	butter	125 mL
1/4 cup	finely chopped parsley leaves	50 mL
2 tbsp	freshly squeezed lemon juice	25 mL
1 tsp	puréed garlic	5 mL
	Freshly ground black pepper	

1. Using a knife, slit the shrimp shells along the back, removing the vein but leaving the shell intact. Set aside.

2. *Brine:* In a large heatproof non-reactive bowl, combine salt and boiling water. Stir until salt dissolves. Add cold water and stir well. Add enough ice cubes to cool the mixture to room temperature.

3. Place shrimp in the brining solution, adding additional cold water, if necessary, to cover. Cover bowl and refrigerate for 30 minutes to 1 hour.

4. Remove shrimp from brine. Discard brine. Rinse shrimp under cold running water and pat dry with paper towel. Brush liberally with olive oil. Thread onto the kabob rods and load onto the gear wheels with the spring ends on the right, or according to the manufacturer's instructions for rotation. Cook until the shells are very pink and the shrimp are cooked through, 10 to 15 minutes.

5. *Parsley Lemon Butter:* Meanwhile, in a small saucepan over medium heat, melt butter. Remove from heat and stir in parsley, lemon juice, garlic and pepper, to taste. Spoon into individual serving bowls and serve alongside the shrimp.

Here are three other sauces to enjoy with these shrimp instead of the Parsley Lemon Butter.

Additional Dipping Sauces for Shrimp

Creole Sauce

1/4 cup	butter	50 mL
1 tbsp	Worcestershire sauce	15 mL
1 tsp	freshly squeezed lemon juice	5 mL
1/2 tsp	hot pepper sauce or to taste	2 mL
	Freshly ground black pepper	

1. In a small saucepan over medium heat, melt butter. Remove from heat and stir in Worcestershire sauce, lemon juice, hot pepper sauce and pepper, to taste.

Lemon Dill Sauce

1/4 cup	freshly squeezed lemon juice	50 mL
2 tbsp	finely chopped dill	25 mL
1 tsp	puréed garlic	5 mL
	Salt and freshly ground black pepper	
1/2 cup	extra virgin olive oil	125 mL

1. In a bowl, combine lemon juice, dill, garlic and salt and pepper, to taste. Gradually whisk in olive oil until blended.

Vietnamese Dipping Sauce

4	cloves garlic, minced	4
2	long red or green chili peppers, minced	2
1/4 cup	fish sauce	50 mL
1/4 cup	water	50 mL
1/4 cup	rice vinegar	50 mL
1/4 cup	granulated sugar	50 mL
1/4 cup	freshly squeezed lime juice	50 mL

1. In a saucepan, combine garlic, chilies, fish sauce, water, vinegar and sugar. Bring the mixture just to the boiling point over medium heat. Do not boil. Remove from heat and stir in lime juice. Refrigerate until ready to use, for up to 2 days.

Rock Lobster Tails with Piri-Piri Butter

SERVES 4

Rock lobster tails, a rare treat, are in many ways more enjoyable to cook and eat than their relatives, whole Maine lobsters. The meaty tail is the only part of this variety that is sold, and it is usually fried or grilled — never steamed or boiled. I find it's particularly good cooked on the rotisserie as it doesn't dry out as much as it does on the barbecue. The less done to this rich, flavorful meat the better. If you don't like the flavor of hot peppers, serve with plain clarified butter.

Tips

I like the bit of heat that chili oil adds to the lobster, but if you're heat averse, by all means use plain olive oil. A flavored oil, such as lemon or oregano oil, would also work well in this recipe.

To make this amount of clarified butter: Cook ¾ cup (175 mL) unsalted butter over low heat, without stirring, until it stops spitting. Carefully pour the clear liquid into a serving dish, leaving the white mild solids behind. Discard the solids.

4	lobster tails, each 8 oz (250 g), thawed if frozen	4
Brine		
¼ cup	kosher salt	50 mL
2	dried red chili peppers	2
1 cup	boiling water	250 mL
4 cups	cold water (approx.)	1 L
	Ice cubes	
¼ cup	chili or olive oil (see Tips, left)	50 mL
Piri-Piri Butter		
½ cup	clarified butter (see Tips, left)	125 mL
2 tsp	piri-piri or other hot pepper sauce	10 mL

1. Using kitchen shears, make a lengthwise cut through the top shell of each lobster tail. Then use a chef's knife to slice through the meat and the bottom shell, cutting the tails in half but leaving the shells intact.

2. *Brine:* In a large heatproof non-reactive bowl, combine salt, chili peppers and boiling water. Stir until the salt dissolves. Add cold water and enough ice cubes to cool the solution to room temperature. Add lobster tails and additional cold water, if necessary, to cover. Cover bowl and refrigerate for 30 minutes.

3. Remove lobster from brine. Discard brine. Rinse lobster under cold running water and pat dry with paper towel. Brush both sides of tails with chili oil. Place side by side in rotisserie basket, close lid tightly and load onto the spit rod assembly. Cook until the shells are very pink and the lobster is cooked through, about 25 minutes.

4. *Piri-Piri Butter:* Meanwhile, in a small bowl, combine clarified butter and piri-piri sauce. Use as a dipping sauce for the lobster.

Vegetables

Roasting in the rotisserie oven is one of my favorite ways of cooking vegetables. Not only do roasted vegetables make a great side dish, but they can also be used as the basic ingredient for other recipes, such as salads, spreads or dips. With a rotisserie oven, roasting vegetables is easy, and the results are delicious. Roasting intensifies the flavor of the vegetables and, once roasted, most do not require additional fat.

To roast vegetables in the rotisserie oven, place them in the rotisserie basket or thread onto the kabob rods. I prefer to brush them with olive oil, which keeps them moist, or melted butter, which also encourages browning, but if you're concerned about fat, you can skip this step. If you're using the rotisserie basket, fill in any empty spaces with crumpled-up foil to ensure the vegetables fit snugly; they shrink when roasted and can easily fall out while the basket turns. Season cooked vegetables with salt, freshly ground black pepper and, if desired, a sprinkling of your favorite fresh herb, such as parsley, chives or thyme, for a finishing touch.

Most vegetables roast well. I've included recipes for my favorites, but I've also had success with leeks, fennel and eggplant. Success depends on getting the timing right. As a general rule of thumb, root vegetables, such as beets, potatoes and parsnips, take longer than more delicate ones, such as zucchini and mushrooms. If you're adapting a recipe for oven-roasted vegetables to the rotisserie, increase the time by about 50 per cent as the rotisserie cooks vegetables at a much lower temperature than the oven.

Skewered vegetables
Spear vegetable pieces (or if they are small enough, just leave them whole as we've done with these beets — onions and small potatoes work well, too) on the horizontal on the kabob rod. Load rods onto the gear wheels with the spring ends on the right.

Roasted Onions

SERVES 4

*Roasted onions are versatile and delicious and, I've always found, greatly appreciated by my guests, who rarely think to serve them as a vegetable. When cooking them on the rotisserie, you can use the basket or the kabob rods. I prefer to brush them liberally with olive oil before cooking, but if you're concerned about fat, you can roast them **au naturel**. On their own, they make a great accompaniment to grilled meats.*

2	sweet onions, such as Vidalia or red onions	2
2 tbsp	extra virgin olive oil or melted butter	25 mL
	Salt and freshly ground black pepper	

Kabob Method

1. Cut each onion into quarters on the vertical and brush all sides of the wedges with olive oil. Spear the pieces on the horizontal on the kabob rod, ensuring that the rod captures all layers of the onion. Load rods onto the gear wheels with the spring ends on the right, or according to the manufacturer's instructions for rotation. Cook until softened and brown, about 1 hour. Remove from rods and season with salt and pepper, to taste, or use in Balsamic-Glazed Onions or Asian-Glazed Onions (see recipes, page 148).

Rotisserie Basket Method

1. Cut each onion in half on the horizontal and brush all sides with olive oil. Place in the rotisserie basket, close lid tightly and load onto the spit rods. (Be sure to place crumpled foil in the corners so the onions fit snugly and don't move around or fall out when rotating.) Cook until the onion softens and begins to brown, about 1 hour. Season with salt and pepper, to taste.

Variation

Herb-Roasted Red Onions: Substitute 2 or 3 red onions for the Vidalia onions. When they have finished cooking, transfer to a small bowl and toss with 1 tbsp (15 mL) fresh thyme leaves, 2 tbsp (25 mL) olive oil and salt and pepper, to taste. For a great side dish, combine with roasted sweet potatoes or carrots.

Balsamic-Glazed Onions

SERVES 4

Simple but delicious, these balsamic-flavored onions make a great accompaniment to roasted poultry and meat.

1	recipe Roasted Onions (see recipe, page 147)	1
1 tbsp	balsamic vinegar	15 mL
1 tsp	packed brown sugar	5 mL
2 tbsp	melted butter	25 mL
	Salt and black pepper	

1. In a small bowl, combine balsamic vinegar and brown sugar, stirring until sugar dissolves. Stir in melted butter until blended. Pour over warm onions and toss to combine. Season with salt and pepper, to taste.

> **Variation**
>
> *Asian-Glazed Onions:* Substitute the following for the balsamic mixture. In a small bowl, combine 2 tbsp (25 mL) rice vinegar, 1 tbsp (15 mL) each soy sauce and vegetable oil. Stir to blend. Season with salt and freshly ground black pepper, to taste. Pour over Roasted Onions and toss.

Roasted Garlic

SERVES 2

Serve Roasted Garlic whole as a side dish (separate into cloves and give each person half a head) or transform it into a tasty spread that can also be used to enhance soups, sauces and stews (see Variation).

Tip

Roast garlic in the rotisserie basket along with other vegetables that have a similar cooking time.

1	whole head garlic, top sliced off	1
2 tbsp	extra virgin olive oil	25 mL

1. In a bowl, combine garlic and olive oil. Toss well. Place in rotisserie basket, close lid tightly and load onto the spit rod assembly. (Place crumpled foil in the basket to ensure that the garlic fits snugly.) Cook until soft and lightly browned, about 35 minutes.

> **Variation**
>
> *Roasted Garlic Spread:* Pop cloves out of their skins and mash with about ½ tsp (2 mL) extra virgin olive oil. Season with salt and pepper, to taste. Covered tightly, it will keep in the refrigerator for up to 1 week.

Roasted Beets

SERVES 4

In my opinion, roasting is the optimum way to maximize the delicious flavor of this versatile vegetable. Beets are extremely easy to prepare in a rotisserie oven and can be served simply as a vegetable side dish with butter, salt, pepper and perhaps a splash of good vinegar. They are also delicious cold in salads.

Tip

Use smaller beets in the rotisserie as they can be cooked whole in their skins. Because larger beets need to be halved, much of their delicious juice is lost during cooking.

8	small beets, root ends intact, stem ends trimmed to ½ inch (1 cm)	8
2 tbsp	olive oil	25 mL

1. Scrub beets thoroughly and pat dry. Brush with olive oil. Thread beets onto 4 kabob rods, leaving space between them to allow the heat to circulate (3 beets per rod). Load rods onto the gear wheels with the spring ends on the right, or according to the manufacturer's instructions for rotation. Roast until the beets are tender enough to be pierced with the tip of a sharp knife but still hold their shape, about 1 hour. Remove from rods. Let cool until they are comfortable to the touch. The skins should lift off easily.

Roasted Maple Beets

SERVES 4

If your taste buds have grown tired of the same old same old, try this. It's an intriguing blend of flavors and makes a particularly nice accompaniment to pork.

1	recipe Roasted Beets (see recipe, above)	1
2 tbsp	whipping (35%) cream	25 mL
1 tbsp	Dijon mustard	15 mL
1 tbsp	apple cider vinegar	15 mL
1 tbsp	pure maple syrup	15 mL
	Salt and freshly ground black pepper	

1. Peel beets and slice thinly.

2. In a serving bowl, combine cream, mustard, vinegar and maple syrup. Mix well. Add beets and toss until thoroughly coated. Chill well before serving.

Beet and Feta Salad

SERVES 4

I particularly like the combination of beets with feta cheese in this tasty salad.

Tip

Take care when spearing beets on the kabob rods as they are very dense. Place them on a cutting board and press down on the rod until it pierces the beet. Then grab the beet and push it down the rod.

1	recipe Roasted Beets (see recipe, page 149)	1
½ cup	finely chopped celery	125 mL
¼ cup	oil and vinegar dressing	50 mL
1 tsp	freshly squeezed lemon juice, optional	5 mL
3 cups	mixed salad greens	750 mL
2 oz	crumbled feta cheese, about ½ cup (125 mL)	60 g

1. Peel beets and cut into ½-inch (1 cm) cubes.

2. In a salad bowl, combine beets, celery, oil and vinegar dressing and lemon juice, if using. Cover and chill thoroughly. Add salad greens and toss well. Sprinkle cheese over top and serve immediately.

Variation

Roasted Beet and Avocado Salad: Omit feta and celery. Add ¼ cup (50 mL) finely chopped green onion and 1 avocado, cut into ½-inch (1 cm) cubes. Add the avocado just before tossing the greens to prevent oxidation.

Roasted Beet and Celery Salad

SERVES 4

This simple salad looks beautiful on a buffet table.

1	recipe Roasted Beets (see recipe, page 149)	1
2 tbsp	oil and vinegar dressing	25 mL
2 tbsp	mayonnaise	25 mL
1 tsp	prepared horseradish, optional	5 mL
4 cups	sliced celery	1 L
	Salt and freshly ground black pepper	

1. Peel beets and cut into ½-inch (1 cm) cubes.

2. In a small bowl, combine oil and vinegar dressing, mayonnaise and horseradish, if using. Set aside.

3. In a salad bowl, combine beets and celery. Add mayonnaise mixture and toss until well combined. Season with salt and pepper, to taste. Chill well before serving.

Roasted Beet, Corn and Goat Cheese Salad

SERVES 4

Here's a visually appealing salad that tastes as good as it looks.

1	recipe Roasted Beets (see recipe, page 149)	1
1 tbsp	balsamic vinegar	15 mL
	Salt and freshly ground black pepper	
3 tbsp	extra virgin olive oil	45 mL
1 cup	corn kernels	250 mL
¼ cup	crumbled soft goat cheese, about 2 oz (60 g)	50 mL

1. Peel beets and cut into ½-inch (1 cm) cubes.

2. In a small bowl, combine balsamic vinegar and salt and pepper, to taste. Stir until salt is dissolved. Gradually whisk in olive oil until blended. Set aside.

3. In a serving bowl, combine beets and corn kernels. Add balsamic mixture and toss well. Sprinkle goat cheese over top and toss to blend. Chill well before serving.

Roasted Carrots

SERVES 4

If you can find them, roast a tricolor combination of carrots, which makes for a very pretty presentation.

Tip

When roasting carrots on the rotisserie, leave them whole to ensure they don't fall out of the rotisserie basket.

2 lbs	sweet carrots, peeled	1 kg
2 tbsp	melted butter	25 mL
	Salt	

1. Brush carrots on all sides with melted butter. Season with salt, to taste. Place in the rotisserie basket, close lid tightly and load onto the spit rod assembly. (Be sure to place crumpled foil in the basket to ensure that the carrots fit snugly and don't move around or fall out when rotating.) Cook until the carrots are browning and tender when pierced with a fork, about 1 hour.

Orange-Glazed Carrots and Onions

SERVES 4

Your taste buds will appreciate this delicious combination. It makes a particularly tasty accompaniment for roast pork.

Tip

If you're cooking your main course on the rotisserie, cover the vegetables and leave them in the saucepan after coating them with the glaze. Reheat for a few minutes when the rest of your dinner is ready, then add the garnish.

1	recipe Roasted Carrots (see recipe, above)	1
1 tbsp	freshly squeezed lemon juice	15 mL
1 tbsp	orange marmalade	15 mL
1 tbsp	pure maple syrup or liquid honey	15 mL
1	recipe Roasted Onions (see recipe, page 147)	1
	Salt and freshly ground black pepper	
	Finely chopped parsley or chives, optional	

1. Cut carrots into ½-inch (1 cm) pieces.

2. In a saucepan over medium heat, combine lemon juice, marmalade and maple syrup. Cook, stirring, until marmalade melts.

3. Add carrots and onions and toss until well coated. Season with salt and pepper, to taste. Transfer to a serving bowl and garnish with parsley, if using.

Roasted Carrot and Lentil Salad

SERVES 4

Here's a delicious and versatile salad with a Middle Eastern feel. It can be used as a main course or on a buffet table, and can even be transformed into a dip.

Tip

Roasted vegetables are particularly tasty when cooked in the speed basket, as they cook closer to the heat source and become more browned. If you have this accessory, reduce the cooking time to about 40 minutes, until the carrots are browning and tender.

1	recipe Roasted Carrots (see recipe, page 152)	1
1	can lentils (14 to 19 oz/398 to 540 mL), drained and rinsed	1
¼ cup	finely chopped green onion	50 mL
¼ cup	oil and vinegar dressing	50 mL
10	black olives, pitted and coarsely chopped	10
1 tbsp	minced garlic	15 mL
	Finely chopped parsley, optional	

1. Cut carrots into ½-inch (1 cm) pieces.
2. In a serving bowl, combine carrots, lentils, green onion, oil and vinegar dressing, olives and garlic. Toss well. Garnish with parsley, if using. Serve at room temperature or chill.

Variation

Carrot Lentil Dip: If you prefer, combine the ingredients in a food processor and process until smooth. Garnish with parsley and additional sliced black olives. Serve with bread or crackers.

Roasted Parsnips

SERVES 4

Sweet and a little bit different, parsnips make a nice change from more traditional root vegetables. They roast particularly well and make a delicious accompaniment for roast chicken or pork. They also combine well with carrots — try a blend of the two with your next holiday turkey.

2 lbs	parsnips, peeled	1 kg
2 tbsp	melted butter	25 mL
	Salt	

1. Brush parsnips all over with melted butter. Season with salt, to taste. Place in rotisserie basket, close lid tightly and load onto spit rod assembly. (Be sure to place crumpled foil in the basket to ensure that the parsnips fit snugly and don't move around or fall out when rotating.) Cook until parsnips are tender when pierced with a fork, about 1 hour.

Salt-Crusted New Potatoes

SERVES 4

Here's a delightfully different way to cook new potatoes. Make more than you think you'll need as requests for seconds are likely.

2 lbs	small new potatoes, skin on	1 kg
1/4 cup	extra virgin olive oil	50 mL
2 tsp	coarse sea salt, crushed	10 mL
	Freshly ground black pepper	

1. Scrub potatoes and pat dry with paper towel.

2. In a large bowl, combine olive oil, salt and pepper, to taste. Add potatoes and toss until thoroughly coated.

3. Thread potatoes onto the kabob rods, leaving space between the pieces to allow the heat to circulate. Load rods onto the gear wheels with spring ends on the right, or according to the manufacturer's instruction for rotation. Cook until potatoes are browning and tender when pierced with the end of a sharp knife but still hold their shape, about 1 hour.

Roasted Potato Wedges

SERVES 4 TO 6

These tasty potatoes make a great snack as well as a vegetable course. I've also used them for dipping, served with a hot cheese dip.

3	baking potatoes, each cut into 6 wedges	3
1/4 cup	extra virgin olive oil	50 mL
	Salt and freshly ground black pepper	

1. In a bowl, combine potatoes, olive oil and salt and pepper, to taste. Toss until potatoes are well coated with oil. Place in rotisserie basket, close lid tightly and load onto the spit rod assembly. (Be sure to place crumpled foil in the basket to ensure that the potatoes fit snugly and don't move around or fall out when rotating.) Cook until potatoes are tender and browned, about 1 hour.

Roasted Peppers

SERVES 4 TO 6

Roasting peppers in the rotisserie has become my preferred method because the flavor of the vegetable dominates, not the charred taste, and it's so convenient. Just set the timer and half an hour later you have perfectly roasted peppers. You don't need to turn them or keep a close eye on them in case they burn.

| 4 to 6 | red, orange or yellow bell peppers | 4 to 6 |

1. Cut peppers in half on the vertical and seed and devein.
2. Arrange pepper halves in the rotisserie basket, skin side up, close lid tightly and load onto the spit rod assembly. (Be sure to place crumpled foil in the basket to ensure that the peppers fit snugly and don't move around or fall out when rotating.) Roast until the skins are blistered and lightly charred, about 30 minutes.
3. Transfer peppers to a heatproof bowl, cover with a plate and let stand for 10 minutes. Using a sharp knife, lift off the skins and discard.

Roasted Red Pepper Dip

MAKES ABOUT 1¾ CUPS (425 ML)

This tasty dip is a staple at our house.

Tip

Lower-fat feta produces a drier dip. If your results seem dry, add 1 tsp (5 mL) or so extra virgin olive oil and pulse.

| 2 | peeled roasted red peppers (see recipe, above) | 2 |
| 8 oz | creamy feta cheese, about 26% M.F. (see Tip, left) | 250 g |

1. In a food processor, combine peppers and cheese and process until smooth. Serve with crudités, crackers or pumpernickel rounds.

Marinated Roasted Peppers

SERVES 6 TO 8

These peppers look beautiful as part of a buffet or make a great accompaniment to roasted meats and fish. They can be enjoyed any time of the year but are particularly easy to make during the summer, when garden-fresh peppers are plentiful and economical.

Tip

Use red, orange or yellow peppers in this recipe. For a particularly attractive presentation, use a combination of all three.

1	recipe Roasted Peppers (see recipe, page 155), using 6 peppers	1
4	cloves garlic, peeled and thinly sliced	4
	Coarsely ground sea salt and freshly ground black pepper	
½ cup	extra virgin olive oil	125 mL
2 tbsp	finely chopped parsley, optional	25 mL
2 tbsp	toasted pine nuts, optional	25 mL
1 tbsp	drained capers, optional	15 mL

1. On a cutting board, cut each peeled half pepper into 4 to 6 strips, on the vertical, and place in a long shallow dish. Sprinkle garlic over top. Season with salt and pepper, to taste. Drizzle oil over top. Cover and refrigerate for 4 hours or overnight.

2. When ready to serve, drain off oil and discard garlic. Garnish peppers with parsley, pine nuts and/or capers, if using.

Roasted Mushrooms

SERVES 6 TO 8

Roasted mushrooms make a great addition to salads, soups and stews.

Tip

When using smaller mushrooms, such as white, cremini, oyster or shiitake, for roasting, cut the stems off close to the cap and save them for making stock. White mushrooms take about 20 minutes, most other varieties about 25. Shiitake take the longest, about 30 minutes.

¼ cup	olive oil	50 mL
½ tsp	salt	2 mL
2 lbs	mushrooms, stems removed (see Tip, left)	1 kg

1. In a bowl, combine olive oil and salt. Add mushroom caps and toss until well coated. Place in the rotisserie basket, close lid tightly and load onto the spit rod assembly. (Be sure to place crumpled foil in the basket to ensure that the mushrooms fit snugly and don't move around or fall out when rotating.) Cook until mushrooms are browned, 20 to 30 minutes, depending upon the variety (see Tip, left).

Roasted Shiitake Mushroom Salad

SERVES 4

Shiitake mushrooms are a particularly versatile mushroom and adapt well to any cooking method. They excel when roasted in the rotisserie.

1 lb	shiitake mushrooms, stems removed	500 g
2 tbsp	olive oil	25 mL

Vinaigrette

2 tbsp	rice vinegar	25 mL
1 tbsp	soy sauce	15 mL
1 tbsp	vegetable oil	15 mL
	Salt and freshly ground black pepper	
4 cups	mixed salad greens	1 L
	Finely chopped parsley or chives, optional	

1. In a bowl, combine mushrooms and olive oil. Toss until mushrooms are coated. Place in rotisserie basket, close lid tightly and load onto the spit rod assembly. (Be sure to place crumpled foil in the basket to ensure that the mushrooms fit snugly and don't move around or fall out when rotating.) Cook until mushrooms are nicely browned, about 30 minutes.

2. *Vinaigrette:* In a bowl, combine rice vinegar, soy sauce and vegetable oil. Add roasted mushrooms and toss to combine. Season with salt and pepper, to taste.

3. Place salad greens in a serving bowl and arrange mushrooms over top. Garnish with parsley or chives, if using.

Warm Mushroom and Pepper Salad

SERVES 4

This tasty salad makes a great main course for four, served with crusty rolls. If you're serving more people, use it as a side or appetizer course to accompany a more substantial meal.

Tips

If you prefer, substitute 16 or so cremini mushrooms for the portobellos. Be sure to place crumbled foil in the corners to ensure the mushrooms fit snugly. Otherwise, they might fall out during roasting.

In my experience, peppers roasted in the rotisserie oven do not get blackened as they do on a barbecue. However, they are just as tasty and, if left to "sweat" for an appropriate time after cooking, will disengage their skins just as easily.

4	large portobello mushrooms (see Tips, left)	4
1	red or yellow bell pepper	1
Vinaigrette		
2	shallots, coarsely chopped	2
2 tbsp	red wine vinegar	25 mL
1 tbsp	chopped parsley	15 mL
2 tsp	Dijon mustard	10 mL
	Salt and freshly ground black pepper	
½ cup	extra virgin olive oil	125 mL
4 cups	mixed salad greens	1 L
¼ cup	crumbled soft goat cheese, about 2 oz (60 g)	50 mL
¼ cup	toasted pine nuts	50 mL

1. Remove stems from mushrooms and scrape gills. Cut bell pepper in half on the vertical, seed and devein. Set aside.

2. *Vinaigrette:* In a food processor or mini-chopper, combine shallots, vinegar, parsley, mustard and salt and pepper, to taste. Process until shallots are very finely chopped and integrated into the mixture. Add olive oil and process until blended.

3. Spoon out 2 tbsp (25 mL) of the vinaigrette and brush over mushroom tops. Set remainder aside.

4. Place mushrooms and bell peppers in the rotisserie basket, top sides up, close lid tightly and load onto the spit rod assembly. (Be sure to place crumpled foil in the basket so the vegetables fit snugly and don't move around or fall out when rotating.) Cook until mushrooms are browned and pepper skins have blistered, about 30 minutes. Place peppers in a heatproof bowl and cover tightly with a plate or plastic wrap. Let stand for 10 minutes. Transfer mushrooms to a cutting board.

5. Arrange salad greens on a deep platter or wide shallow bowl. Drizzle a bit of vinaigrette over mushrooms and slice thinly. Arrange over top of the greens. Remove peppers from the bowl and gently lift off the skins. Slice thinly on the vertical and arrange attractively alongside the mushrooms. Pour the rest of the vinaigrette over the salad, covering the exposed greens as well as the mushrooms and peppers. Sprinkle with goat cheese and pine nuts. Serve immediately.

Roasted Zucchini

SERVES 4

Roasted and tossed with fresh thyme leaves or chives, zucchini makes a lovely accompaniment to roast meat or fish.

2	medium zucchini	2
2 tbsp	olive oil	25 mL
1 tsp	coarse sea salt, crushed	5 mL
	Freshly ground black pepper	
	Extra virgin olive oil, optional	
	Fresh thyme leaves or finely chopped chives, optional	

1. Peel zucchini, if desired, and cut into 1-inch (2.5 cm) slices.

2. In a bowl, combine olive oil, salt and pepper, to taste. Add zucchini and toss to combine. Thread onto kabob rods and load onto the gear wheels with spring ends on the right, or according to the manufacturer's instructions for rotation. Cook until tender, about 30 minutes. Drizzle with extra virgin olive oil and sprinkle with thyme leaves, if using.

Roasted Sweet Potatoes

SERVES 4

Try these — they make a delicious accompaniment to any roast meat.

Tip

If you prefer, cut each potato into 6 wedges, brush with butter, and place in the rotisserie basket. Cook until tender, about 1 hour.

4	sweet potatoes	4
2 tbsp	melted butter	25 mL

1. Peel sweet potatoes and cut into 1-inch (2.5 cm) slices.

2. Brush potato slices with butter. Thread onto kabob rods, leaving space between them to allow the heat to circulate. Place on gear wheel assembly with spring ends on the right, or according to the manufacturer's instructions for rotation. Cook until tender, about 1 hour.

> **Variation**
> Add ½ tsp (2 mL) curry powder and/or 2 tsp (10 mL) brown sugar to the melted butter if you prefer.

Salmon with Peperonata (page 124)

Roasted Corn

SERVES 4 TO 6

Roasted corn is particularly delicious and flavorful. Although the easiest way to roast corn is in the rotisserie basket, most cobs are too thick to fit in the standard basket. If your rotisserie oven offers the option, you can invest in the giant basket. Alternatively, you can cook the corn on the kabob rods. It takes a bit of effort to skewer the cobs on the rods, but the results are delicious.

Tip

Cutting the ends of the cobs flat allows you to place the cob on a cutting board and use pressure and gravity to force the skewer through. Be careful when you're doing this as you don't want to pierce your hand with the rod.

| 6 | ears fresh corn on the cob | 6 |

1. Gently pull back the husks of each cob, without detaching, and remove all the silk. If cooking on the kabob rods, cut off a small piece on both ends of every cob to create a flat surface (see Tip, left). Fill the sink with lukewarm water and thoroughly soak the corn for about 20 minutes.

2. Remove corn from water and return husks to their original position, enclosing the cob. Arrange corn in the rotisserie basket or thread each piece onto a kabob rod. Cook until corn is tender and juicy, about 30 minutes. Watch carefully, especially toward the end of the cooking time, as the husks have a tendency to burn. Remove from kabob rods. Remove husks and serve with plain or flavored butter (see recipes, page 59).

Pancetta-Wrapped Trout
(page 134, Variation)

Roasted Tomatoes

SERVES 4

Although most tomatoes are too large to fit whole into the rotisserie basket, Roma tomatoes are an exception. They roast quite nicely on the rotisserie and go particularly well with chicken or beef.

¼ cup	extra virgin olive oil	50 mL
½ tsp	salt	2 mL
8	Roma (plum) tomatoes	8
	Extra virgin olive oil	
	Sea salt and freshly ground black pepper	
	Finely chopped parsley or chives, optional	

1. In a bowl, combine olive oil and salt. Add tomatoes and toss until coated.

2. Place tomatoes in rotisserie basket, close lid tightly and load onto the spit rod assembly. (Be sure to place crumpled foil in the basket to ensure that the tomatoes fit snugly and don't move around or fall out when rotating.) Cook until their skins start to blister and they begin to char, about 40 minutes.

3. Remove tomatoes from basket and place in a serving bowl. Serve them whole, drizzled with extra virgin olive oil. Season with sea salt and pepper, to taste. Garnish with parsley, if using.

Second Acts

One of the benefits of rotisserie cooking is that you're likely to have leftovers. I say "benefits" because if you have some cold roast chicken in the refrigerator, you've already cooked the main ingredient and are well on your way to having dinner prepared for the following night. Since this is a boon to time-starved cooks, I've included a smattering of recipes that transform leftover chicken, turkey, beef, lamb, salmon and shrimp into another delicious dish. These will get you started, and I'm sure you have a few ideas of your own. My only caveat is to make sure that none of the flavorings in the original recipe clash with the one using leftovers. This isn't a problem with most of the chicken recipes since you can remove the skin, where the seasonings are concentrated, but it might, for instance, be an issue with the salmon recipes, where the flavorings are likely to be more integrated.

Chicken Salad Amandine

SERVES 4

This old-fashioned recipe, which is a great way to use up leftover chicken, has wide appeal. It makes a delicious luncheon dish or a light one-course dinner. The quantity of dressing may seem substantial for the amount of chicken, but it also dresses the salad greens.

Tip

To toast almonds: In a dry nonstick skillet over medium heat, stir almonds constantly until golden brown, 3 to 4 minutes. Immediately transfer to a small bowl to prevent burning.

¼ cup	mayonnaise	50 mL
2 tbsp	extra virgin olive oil	25 mL
2 tbsp	freshly squeezed lemon juice	25 mL
½ tsp	salt	2 mL
	Freshly ground black pepper	
4 cups	cubed cooked chicken, skin removed, about ½-inch (1 cm) cubes	1 L
½ cup	finely chopped celery	125 mL
2 tbsp	finely chopped red or green onion	25 mL
4 cups	torn salad greens, such as hearts of romaine or lettuce, washed and dried	1 L
2 tbsp	toasted slivered or sliced almonds (see Tip, left)	25 mL

1. In a bowl, combine mayonnaise, olive oil, lemon juice, salt and black pepper, to taste.

2. In a separate bowl, combine chicken, celery and onion. Add mayonnaise mixture. Toss to combine.

3. Spread salad greens over a deep platter. Spoon chicken mixture on top. Garnish with almonds and serve immediately.

Variation

Chicken Salad Sandwich: Omit the salad greens and almonds. Reduce the quantity of mayonnaise, olive oil and lemon juice by half and use the chicken mixture as a filling for sandwiches. Add sliced tomato, lettuce and/or cucumber slices, as desired.

Cobb Salad

SERVES 4

Until I actually tasted one, I thought that a Cobb salad contained corn, which is probably an easy mistake to make. Actually, this American classic is named for Bob Cobb, the restaurateur who invented it. It makes a great luncheon or light dinner dish and is extremely nutritious.

Tips

The hint of walnuts in the walnut oil adds a flavorful dimension to this salad, but if you don't have walnut oil, the salad will still be delicious. Just use an extra tablespoon (15 mL) olive oil instead.

Save any leftover vinaigrette and use in another salad.

Vinaigrette

2 tbsp	white wine vinegar	25 mL
1/2 tsp	salt	2 mL
	Freshly ground black pepper	
1/3 cup	extra virgin olive oil	75 mL
1 tbsp	walnut oil (see Tips, left)	15 mL
4 cups	torn romaine lettuce (bite-size pieces), washed and dried	1 L
2 cups	cubed cooked chicken or turkey, skin removed, about 1/2-inch (1 cm) cubes	500 mL
1 cup	arugula	250 mL
1	small red onion, thinly sliced	1
1	avocado, peeled, pitted and cut into 1/2-inch (1 cm) cubes	1
16	cherry tomatoes	16
4	hard-cooked eggs, peeled and quartered	4
4 oz	crisp cooked bacon, crumbled	125 g
3 oz	blue cheese, crumbled, about 1/3 cup (75 mL)	90 g

1. *Vinaigrette:* In a bowl, combine vinegar, salt and pepper, to taste. Stir well until salt dissolves. Whisk in olive and walnut oils. Set aside.

2. On a deep platter or serving bowl, spread lettuce evenly. Layer chicken, arugula, red onion, avocado and tomatoes over top. Arrange eggs around the edges. Sprinkle bacon and blue cheese evenly over top. Drizzle with vinaigrette and serve.

Chicken Curry

Don't Reheat

SERVES 4

This delicious one-pan dinner is one of my favorite ways to use up leftover chicken. I like to serve it with mango chutney.

Tip

For a change, cook 2 small chickens on the rotisserie simultaneously, eat one immediately and refrigerate the other to make this delicious curry. Simply cut it into pieces, leaving the meat on the bones but removing skin if the flavors conflict with curry.

1 tbsp	vegetable oil	15 mL
½ cup	diced onion	125 mL
1 tbsp	all-purpose flour	15 mL
2 tsp	curry powder	10 mL
1 cup	chicken stock	250 mL
2 cups	cubed cooked chicken, skin removed, about 1-inch (2.5 cm) cubes, or cut-up chicken (see Tip, left)	500 mL
½ cup	green peas or red bell pepper strips	125 mL
	Salt and freshly ground black pepper	
	Hot cooked white rice or Indian bread, such as naan or chapati	

1. In a skillet, heat vegetable oil over medium heat. Add onion and cook, stirring, until softened, about 3 minutes.

2. Add flour and curry powder and cook, stirring, for 1 minute. Add stock. Bring to a boil and cook, stirring, until thickened, about 2 minutes.

3. Add chicken and peas. Cover and simmer until chicken is heated through, about 5 minutes. (If you're using a cut-up rotisserie bone-in chicken, add 5 minutes to the heating time.) Taste and season with salt and pepper, to taste.

4. Serve over hot fluffy rice or with warm Indian bread.

Chicken and Artichoke Bake

SERVES 4

This moist tasty bake has a retro feel and a real hit of tomato flavor. It takes almost no time to prepare and is delicious over hot white rice.

Preheat oven to 350°F (180°C)
6-cup (1.5 L) baking dish, greased

1	can (10 oz/284 mL) condensed cream of tomato soup, undiluted	1
½ cup	mayonnaise	125 mL
1 tbsp	freshly squeezed lemon juice	15 mL
1 tbsp	Dijon mustard	15 mL
1 cup	dry bread crumbs	250 mL
2 tbsp	melted butter	25 mL
2 cups	cubed cooked chicken, skin removed, about 1-inch (2.5 cm) cubes	500 mL
1	can (14 oz/398 mL) artichoke hearts, drained and quartered	1
1½ cups	green peas, thawed if frozen, or 1 can (14 oz/398 mL) green peas, drained	375 mL
2 tbsp	grated Parmesan cheese	25 mL

1. In a bowl, combine soup, mayonnaise, lemon juice and mustard. Set aside.

2. In another bowl, combine bread crumbs and butter.

3. In prepared baking dish, combine chicken, artichoke hearts, peas and reserved soup mixture. Mix to combine. Spread bread crumb mixture evenly over top. Sprinkle Parmesan cheese evenly over crumbs.

4. Bake in preheated oven until top is golden and mixture is bubbling, about 20 minutes.

Chicken Pizza with Red Peppers and Goat Cheese

SERVES 4 TO 6

Although there are times when nothing else will do, the days when pizza meant pepperoni and mushrooms are long past. Here's a delicious pizza that uses leftover roast chicken and other tasty ingredients that couldn't be easier to make.

Tip

When using prepared pizza dough, read the package instructions and adjust this method accordingly. I like to make a thin crust and bake the dough with nothing on it for about 7 minutes. Then I brush the warm crust with the olive oil and pesto and proceed as directed, reducing the remaining cooking time to 8 to 10 minutes. Watch carefully to ensure the edges of the crust don't burn.

Preheat oven to 400°F (200°C)
Baking sheet, lightly greased

1	10-inch (25 cm) pizza crust or prepared pizza dough (see Tip, left)	1
1 tbsp	olive oil	15 mL
1/4 cup	prepared sun-dried tomato pesto	50 mL
1 1/2 cups	finely shredded mozzarella	375 mL
1 cup	thinly sliced cooked chicken, skin removed	250 mL
2	roasted red peppers, chopped	2
4 oz	crumbled soft goat cheese, about 1/2 cup (125 mL)	125 g
	Sliced black olives, optional	
	Sliced red onion, optional	

1. Place crust on prepared baking sheet. Brush with olive oil and sun-dried tomato pesto.

2. Sprinkle mozzarella evenly over top. Arrange chicken evenly over cheese. Sprinkle red pepper then goat cheese evenly over chicken. Top with olives and/or onions, if using.

3. Bake in preheated oven until crust is golden and cheese has melted, 10 to 15 minutes.

> ### Variation
> *Mini Pita Pizzas:* If you don't have a pizza crust, try making mini pizzas with this recipe, using 4 to 6 pita breads. Follow the method above, leaving a 1/2-inch (1 cm) border around the edge of the pita, and reduce the cooking time to about 6 minutes, just until the cheese melts.

Fettuccine Florentine

SERVES 4

I call this Fettuccine Florentine because it contains spinach, which blends beautifully with Alfredo sauce, as well as the traditional Mornay sauce that usually tops "Florentine" dishes.

12 oz	fettuccine	375 g
1 tbsp	vegetable oil	15 mL
½ cup	diced onion	125 mL
2 tsp	minced garlic	10 mL
1	package (10 oz/300 g) spinach, stems removed and coarsely chopped, or 1 package (10 oz/300 g) frozen spinach, thawed	1
1 tbsp	freshly squeezed lemon juice	15 mL
2 cups	cubed cooked chicken, skin removed, about 1-inch (2.5 cm) cubes	500 mL
1½ cups	prepared Alfredo sauce	375 mL

1. Cook pasta in a pot of boiling salted water, until tender to the bite, about 3 minutes if using fresh fettuccine, 5 minutes if dried. Drain.

2. Meanwhile, in a skillet, heat vegetable oil over medium heat. Add onion and cook, stirring, until softened, about 3 minutes. Add garlic and cook, stirring, for 1 minute. Add fresh spinach, in batches if necessary, and cook until wilted. (If using thawed frozen spinach, add with liquid, and cook for 5 minutes). Sprinkle with lemon juice and stir. Add chicken and cook, stirring, until heated through. Add Alfredo sauce and stir well for about 30 seconds or until sauce is hot. Remove from heat.

3. In a warm serving bowl, combine fettuccine and Alfredo mixture. Toss to combine.

Variation
Fettuccine with Sweet Pea Sauce: Substitute 2 cups (500 mL) cooked green peas for the spinach. Toss to combine with the onion mixture after the lemon juice has been added, but do not cook. Add Alfredo sauce and continue as directed.

Orange and Onion Chicken

SERVES 2

This is a great way to get double duty out of rotisserie chicken. Cook two small chickens at a time; use one immediately and refrigerate the other to make this tasty dish for dinner the following day. In addition to any simply seasoned chicken, Herb-Roasted, French Bistro and Chili-Roasted Chicken (see recipes, pages 20, 21 and 24) would work well in this dish. This is great with fluffy white rice.

Tip

You can place the chicken in an oven-to-table baking dish and warm in a preheated oven (350°F/180°C) for 15 minutes. Alternatively, place chicken in a microwave-safe dish, cover and heat on High power until it is heated through, about 5 minutes.

Preheat oven to 350°F (180°C) (see Tip, left)

1	small rotisserie-cooked chicken, quartered	1
1 tbsp	vegetable oil	15 mL
1	red onion, sliced on the vertical	1
1 cup	orange juice	250 mL
½ cup	orange marmalade	125 mL
1 tsp	soy sauce	5 mL
1 tbsp	cornstarch, dissolved in 2 tbsp (25 mL) water	15 mL

1. In a microwave-safe dish or a baking dish, heat chicken until warm (see Tip, left).

2. In a skillet, heat vegetable oil over medium heat. Add onion and cook, stirring, until it begins to glaze, about 3 minutes. Add orange juice, orange marmalade and soy sauce and cook, stirring, until marmalade dissolves and mixture reaches a simmer, about 2 minutes. Add cornstarch mixture and stir just until it thickens (this will happen very quickly). Remove from heat, pour over warm chicken and serve immediately.

Chicken Tacos

SERVES 4

Kids love this messy, tactile dish, and adults enjoy its Tex-Mex flavors and ease of preparation. I've deliberately kept the spicing mild to appeal to young palates, but the heat is easily bumped up with the addition of a jalapeño or chipotle pepper, or spicy salsa.

2 cups	cubed cooked chicken, skin removed, about 1-inch (2.5 cm) cubes	500 mL
½ tsp	chili powder	2 mL
1 cup	drained canned corn kernels or thawed corn kernels	250 mL
1	roasted red pepper, finely chopped	1
1	can (14 oz/398 mL) refried beans	1
1	finely chopped jalapeño pepper or chipotle pepper in adobo sauce, optional	1
	Freshly ground black pepper	
1 cup	shredded Tex-Mex cheese mix or Monterey Jack	250 mL
12	taco shells	12
	Salsa	
	Shredded lettuce	
	Chopped tomato	
	Finely chopped red or green onion	
	Cubed avocado	
	Sour cream	

1. In a saucepan over medium heat, combine chicken, chili powder, corn, roasted red pepper, refried beans and jalapeño pepper, if using. Season with black pepper, to taste. Bring to a boil. Reduce heat to low and simmer until chicken is heated through and mixture is hot, about 3 minutes. Add cheese and stir until melted.

2. Meanwhile, warm taco shells according to package directions.

3. Fill warm shells with bean mixture and garnish with any combination of salsa, lettuce, tomato, onion, avocado and/or sour cream.

Turkey Tetrazzini

SERVES 4

This classic dish, often made with chicken, is not Italian in origin as the name suggests. It was invented in San Francisco, around the turn of the century, to honor the great opera singer Luisa Tetrazzini.

Preheat oven to 350°F (180°C)
10-cup (2.5 L) baking dish, greased

8 oz	small tubular pasta, such as penne or macaroni	250 g
2 tbsp	butter	25 mL
8 oz	sliced mushrooms, about 3 cups (750 mL)	250 g
1 tbsp	vegetable oil	15 mL
1	onion, minced	1
4	cloves garlic, minced	4
½ tsp	dried thyme leaves	2 mL
2 tbsp	all-purpose flour	25 mL
2 cups	chicken or turkey stock	500 mL
¼ cup	sweet sherry, dry white wine or additional stock	50 mL
¼ cup	whipping (35%) cream	50 mL
½ cup	grated Parmesan cheese Salt and freshly ground black pepper	125 mL
1 cup	frozen peas, thawed	250 mL
2 cups	cubed cooked turkey, skin removed, about 1-inch (2.5 cm) cubes	500 mL

Topping

1 cup	dry bread crumbs, such as panko	250 mL
¼ cup	grated Parmesan cheese	50 mL
2 tbsp	melted butter	25 mL

1. Cook pasta in a pot of boiling salted water until tender to the bite, about 8 minutes. Drain and set aside.

2. Meanwhile, in a skillet over medium heat, melt butter. Add mushrooms and cook, stirring, until they lose their liquid and pan is relatively dry, about 8 minutes. Transfer to prepared baking dish and set aside.

3. Return skillet to heat and add vegetable oil. Add onion and cook, stirring, until softened, about 3 minutes. Add garlic and thyme and cook, stirring, for 1 minute. Add flour and cook, stirring, for 1 minute. Add chicken stock and bring to a boil. Cook, stirring, until mixture thickens, about 3 minutes. Stir in sherry, cream and Parmesan. Season with salt and pepper, to taste. Add peas and turkey and stir until heated through. Pour over mushrooms. Add pasta and stir well.

4. *Topping:* In a bowl, combine bread crumbs and Parmesan cheese. Sprinkle evenly over turkey mixture and drizzle with melted butter. Bake in preheated oven until top is browned and mixture is heated through, about 20 minutes.

Variation

Chicken Tetrazzini: Substitute chicken for the turkey.

Southwest Turkey 'n' Rice

SERVES 4 TO 6

Here's a nutritious and flavorful solution to using up leftover turkey. Serve this with a big tossed salad and crusty whole-grain rolls, and expect requests for seconds.

Tip

Ancho and New Mexico chilies are mild to medium-hot chilies widely available in dried form. Guajillo chilies, which have a similar position on the heat scale, would also work well in this recipe.

2	dried ancho or New Mexico chili peppers (see Tip, left)	2
2 cups	boiling water	500 mL
1 tbsp	vegetable oil	15 mL
1	onion, finely chopped	1
4	cloves garlic, minced	4
1 tbsp	cumin seeds, toasted and ground (see Tips, page 120)	15 mL
1/4 tsp	ground cinnamon	1 mL
1 cup	brown rice	250 mL
2 to 3 cups	cubed cooked turkey, skin removed, about 1-inch (2.5 cm) cubes	500 to 750 mL
1 cup	chicken or turkey stock	250 mL
1 tbsp	freshly squeezed lemon or lime juice	15 mL
1	can (28 oz/796 mL) tomatoes, including juice, coarsely chopped	1
	Salt and freshly ground black pepper	
	Finely chopped cilantro or parsley, optional	

1. In a heatproof bowl, soak dried chili peppers in boiling water for 30 minutes. Drain and discard liquid. Remove stems, pat dry, chop finely and set aside.

2. In a heavy pot or Dutch oven with a tight-fitting lid, heat vegetable oil over medium heat. Add onions and cook, stirring, until softened, about 3 minutes. Add garlic, cumin, cinnamon, reserved chilies and rice and cook, stirring, until rice is coated, about 1 minute. Stir in turkey, stock, lemon juice and tomatoes with juice. Season with salt and pepper, to taste. Reduce heat to low. Cover and cook until rice is tender, about 45 minutes. Garnish with cilantro, if using, and serve.

Thai-Style Beef Salad

SERVES 4

A more involved version of this recipe is one of my favorite dishes from Andrew Chase's **Asian Bistro Cookbook.** *I've eaten Andrew's own to-die-for version, made with freshly grilled steak, but leftover roast beef or steak is a delicious alternative. While lime juice is my preference, lemon juice also produces a tasty result. Andrew uses arugula, but bagged mixed salad greens, such as mesclun mix, work well, too.*

Tips

In southeast Asian countries, such as Thailand and Vietnam, fish sauce, which is made from brine-covered and fermented fish, most often anchovies, is used as widely as soy sauce in China and Japan. It's very pungent but lends a distinctive and appealing note to many dishes. It is now available in the Asian food section of many supermarkets.

If using fresh lemongrass, smash it first, discard the outer core and slice it very thinly as it is quite fibrous.

¼ cup	freshly squeezed lime or lemon juice	50 mL
3 tbsp	fish sauce (see Tips, left)	45 mL
2 tsp	minced gingerroot	10 mL
2 tsp	Asian chili sauce	10 mL
¾ cup	thinly sliced roast beef or steak, chopped	175 mL
2 cups	diced peeled cucumber	500 mL
1 cup	thinly sliced red or green onions, white part only	250 mL
4 tbsp	finely chopped cilantro, divided	60 mL
1 tbsp	thinly sliced lemongrass (see Tips, left) or bottled preserved lemongrass (see Tips, page 180) or 1 tsp (5 mL) grated lemon zest	15 mL
4 cups	mixed salad greens or arugula, washed and dried	1 L
12	cherry tomatoes, halved	12

1. In a bowl, combine lime juice, fish sauce, gingerroot and chili sauce. Mix well. Add beef, cucumber, onions, 2 tbsp (25 mL) cilantro and lemongrass. Toss to combine.

2. Spread salad greens over a deep platter or serving plate. Arrange meat mixture on top. Surround with cherry tomatoes and garnish with remaining 2 tbsp (25 mL) cilantro. Serve immediately.

Broccoli, Beef and Cabbage Salad

SERVES 4

This recipe comes from my friend and recipe tester Audrey King, who first tasted it at the Steamboat Inn in southern Oregon, which is one of her family's favorite places to visit. Not only is it a great way to use up leftover beef, it's a delicious and nutritious meal in itself.

Vinaigrette

¼ cup	rice vinegar	50 mL
2 tbsp	soy sauce	25 mL
1	clove garlic, finely minced	1
2 tsp	puréed gingerroot	10 mL
¼ cup	extra virgin olive oil	50 mL
4 cups	broccoli florets	1 L
1 ½ cups	cooked beef, such as roast beef or flank steak, cut into thin strips	375 mL
2 cups	thinly sliced red cabbage	500 mL
2 tbsp	toasted sesame seeds	25 mL

1. *Vinaigrette:* In a bowl, combine vinegar, soy sauce, garlic and gingerroot. Gradually whisk in olive oil. Set aside.

2. In a large pot of boiling salted water, blanch broccoli for 1½ minutes. Drain and immediately plunge into ice water. (The broccoli should be bright green and still crunchy.) Drain again and transfer to a paper towel to dry.

3. In a serving bowl, combine broccoli, beef and red cabbage. Add dressing and toss well. Sprinkle with sesame seeds.

Mediterranean Beef Salad

SERVES 4 TO 6

This salad is so tasty and easy to make that it's likely to become a staple. It's equally delicious made with lamb.

Tip

You can also make this in a small bowl, using a whisk. Just chop the anchovies finely and add the vinegar. Stir well. Then whisk in the olive oil and season to taste.

Vinaigrette

4	anchovy fillets, chopped	4
1 tbsp	red wine vinegar	15 mL
¼ cup	extra virgin olive oil	50 mL
	Salt and freshly ground black pepper	
4 cups	mixed salad greens	1 L
1 cup	thinly sliced roast beef	250 mL

1. *Vinaigrette:* In a mini-chopper or small bowl (see Tip, left), combine anchovies, vinegar and olive oil. Season with salt and pepper, to taste.

2. Spread greens on a large serving plate or platter. Arrange beef over top. Drizzle with vinaigrette and serve.

> ### Variation
> *Mediterranean Lamb Salad:* Substitute an equal quantity of roast lamb for the beef.

Lamb and Pita Salad

SERVES 4 TO 6

I call this my "sandwich in a bowl" salad. It's like a tasty pita pocket that you can eat with a fork.

Vinaigrette

2 tbsp	freshly squeezed lemon juice	25 mL
½ tsp	salt	2 mL
Pinch	dried oregano leaves	Pinch
¼ cup	extra virgin olive oil	50 mL
	Freshly ground black pepper	
1 cup	thinly sliced roast lamb	250 mL
2	pita breads, toasted, each cut into 8 triangles	2
4	green onions, white part only, thinly sliced	4
½ cup	finely chopped parsley	125 mL
4 cups	mixed salad greens	1 L

1. *Vinaigrette:* In a small bowl, combine lemon juice, salt and oregano. Mix well until salt is dissolved. Gradually whisk in olive oil. Season with pepper, to taste, and additional salt, if desired. Set aside.

2. In a bowl, combine lamb, pita, onions, parsley and salad greens. Add vinaigrette and toss well.

Variation
Beef and Pita Salad: Substitute an equal quantity of beef for the lamb.

Shrimp-Stuffed Avocado

SERVES 4 AS AN APPETIZER

This is a great way to use up leftover shrimp. In fact, it's so good I often cook a few extra so I can make it. It's an elegant starter for any meal, and this quantity also makes a delicious and nutritious light dinner for two.

Tips

Refrigerate cooked shrimp in their shells, then peel and chop just before using.

Halve avocados just before using (otherwise the flesh will turn brown). Use the tip of a spoon to remove the pit.

8	large cooked shrimp, peeled and chopped	8
1 tbsp	freshly squeezed lemon juice	15 mL
½ cup	finely chopped celery	125 mL
2 tbsp	finely chopped green onion, white part only	25 mL
2 tbsp	finely chopped dill, optional	25 mL
¼ cup	mayonnaise	50 mL
	Salt and freshly ground black pepper	
2	avocados (see Tips, left)	2

1. In a bowl, combine shrimp and lemon juice. Toss to combine. Add celery, green onion, dill, if using, mayonnaise and salt and pepper, to taste. Mix well. Taste and adjust seasoning.

2. Cut avocados in half and remove pit. Place one half on each plate. Fill with shrimp mixture (it will spill over the sides) and serve immediately.

Thai-Style Salmon Curry

SERVES 2

If, like me, you're fond of Thai food, here's an easy way to taste its unique flavors. Given the popularity of this cuisine, Thai ingredients are now widely available (see Tips, below).

Tips

This recipe can be doubled or tripled.

Canned or frozen peas work well in this curry. If using canned peas, be sure to drain them before adding to the recipe. Cook frozen peas according to package instructions.

Dried lime leaves (available in Asian markets) can be substituted for the lime juice. Use 4 leaves, torn into thirds, and add along with the chili peppers. Remove along with the chilies.

Look for bottled preserved lemongrass and fish sauce in the Asian food section of well-stocked supermarkets.

1	can (14 oz/398 mL) coconut milk	1
1 to 2	fresh chili peppers, minced, or 3 whole dried red chili peppers	1 to 2
1	stick lemongrass, smashed and sliced into 1-inch (2.5 cm) slices, or 2 pieces preserved lemongrass (see Tips, left)	1
1 cup	cooked flaked salmon	250 mL
1 cup	cooked green peas (see Tips, left)	250 mL
2 tbsp	fish sauce	25 mL
2 tbsp	freshly squeezed lemon juice	25 mL
1 tbsp	freshly squeezed lime juice	15 mL
1 tsp	packed brown sugar	5 mL
	Hot white rice or noodles	
½	red bell pepper, seeded and cut into thin slivers, optional	½
	Finely chopped cilantro, optional	

1. In a saucepan over medium heat, combine coconut milk, chili peppers and lemongrass. Bring to a simmer.

2. Add salmon and peas and cook, stirring, being careful not to let the mixture boil, about 3 minutes. Add fish sauce, lemon juice, lime juice and brown sugar and cook, stirring, for 1 minute. Taste for seasoning, adding more fish sauce, lemon or lime juice or brown sugar, if desired.

3. Remove dried peppers and lemongrass. Pour over rice or noodles. Garnish with red pepper slices and cilantro, if using. Serve immediately.

Salmon Burgers

SERVES 2

Nothing says lunch or a quick dinner better than a good burger. Here's a yummy fish-based version that can be easily varied by changing the toppings. To serve more, simply double or triple the recipe.

1 cup	cooked flaked salmon	250 mL
1	egg, beaten	1
1 tsp	dried Italian seasoning	5 mL
1/2 cup	fine dry bread crumbs, divided	125 mL
1/4 tsp	salt	1 mL
	Freshly ground black pepper	
1/4 cup	finely chopped red or green onion, optional	50 mL
2 tbsp	finely chopped bell pepper, optional	25 mL
2 tbsp	vegetable oil	25 mL
2	onion or whole wheat buns, split and toasted	2
	Easy Tartar Sauce (see recipe, below)	
	Lettuce	
	Sliced tomato	
	Sliced red onion	
	Sliced red or yellow bell pepper	

1. In a bowl, combine salmon, egg, Italian seasoning, 1/4 cup (50 mL) bread crumbs, salt, black pepper, to taste, and onion and bell pepper, if using. Mix well. Form mixture into 2 patties, each 1/2 inch (1 cm) thick. Spread remaining bread crumbs on a plate. Dip each patty into crumbs, covering both sides. Discard any excess crumbs.

2. In a nonstick skillet, heat vegetable oil over medium heat. Add patties and cook, turning once, until hot and golden, about 3 minutes per side.

3. Serve on warm buns slathered with tartar sauce and lettuce, tomato, onion and/or bell pepper.

Easy Tartar Sauce

1. In a bowl, combine 1/2 cup (125 mL) mayonnaise with 2 tbsp (25 mL) sweet green pickle relish. Stir to blend.

Library and Archives Canada Cataloguing in Publication

Finlayson, Judith
125 best rotisserie oven recipes / Judith Finlayson.

Includes index.
ISBN 0-7788-0110-1

1. Roasting (Cookery) I. Title. II. Title: One hundred twenty-five best rotisserie oven recipes.

TX690.F55 2005   641.7'1   C2004-906427-4

Index

More Great Books from Robert Rose

Appliance Cooking

- 125 Best Microwave Oven Recipes
  by Johanna Burkhard
- The Blender Bible
  by Andrew Chase and Nicole Young
- 125 Best Pressure Cooker Recipes
  by Cinda Chavich
- The 150 Best Slow Cooker Recipes
  by Judith Finlayson
- Delicious & Dependable Slow Cooker Recipes
  by Judith Finlayson
- 125 Best Vegetarian Slow Cooker Recipes
  by Judith Finlayson
- 125 Best Rotisserie Oven Recipes
  by Judith Finlayson
- The Best Family Slow Cooker Recipes
  by Donna-Marie Pye
- 125 Best Indoor Grill Recipes
  by Ilana Simon
- The Best Convection Oven Cookbook
  by Linda Stephen
- 125 Best Toaster Oven Recipes
  by Linda Stephen
- 250 Best American Bread Machine Baking Recipes
  by Donna Washburn and Heather Butt
- 250 Best Canadian Bread Machine Baking Recipes
  by Donna Washburn and Heather Butt

Baking

- 250 Best Cakes & Pies
  by Esther Brody
- 250 Best Cobblers, Custards, Cupcakes, Bread Puddings & More
  by Esther Brody
- 500 Best Cookies, Bars & Squares
  by Esther Brody
- 500 Best Muffin Recipes
  by Esther Brody
- 125 Best Cheesecake Recipes
  by George Geary
- 125 Best Chocolate Recipes
  by Julie Hasson
- 125 Best Chocolate Chip Recipes
  by Julie Hasson
- 125 Best Cupcakes Recipes
  by Julie Hasson

Healthy Cooking

- 125 Best Vegetarian Recipes
  by Byron Ayanoglu with contributions from Alexis Kemezys
- America's Best Cookbook for Kids with Diabetes
  by Colleen Bartley
- Canada's Best Cookbook for Kids with Diabetes
  by Colleen Bartley
- The Juicing Bible
  by Pat Crocker and Susan Eagles

- The Smoothies Bible
  by Pat Crocker
- 125 Best Vegan Recipes
  by Beth Gurney and Maxine Chuck
- 500 Best Healthy Recipes
  Edited by Lynn Roblin, RD
- 125 Best Gluten-Free Recipes
  by Donna Washburn and Heather Butt
- The Best Gluten-Free Family Cookbook
  by Donna Washburn and Heather Butt

- America's Everyday Diabetes Cookbook
  Edited by Katherine E. Younker, MBA, RD
- Canada's Everyday Diabetes Choice Recipes
  Edited by Katherine E. Younker, MBA, RD
- Canada's Complete Diabetes Cookbook
  Edited by Katherine E. Younker, MBA, RD
- The Best Diabetes Cookbook (U.S.)
  Edited by Katherine E. Younker, MBA, RD
- The Best Low-carb Cookbook
  from Robert Rose

Recent Bestsellers

- The Convenience Cook
  by Judith Finlayson
- 125 Best Ice Cream Recipes
  by Marilyn Linton and Tanya Linton

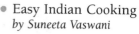

- Easy Indian Cooking
  by Suneeta Vaswani
- Simply Thai Cooking
  by Wandee Young and Byron Ayanoglu

Health

- The Complete Natural Medicine Guide to the 50 Most Common Medicinal Herbs
  by Dr. Heather Boon, B.Sc.Phm., Ph.D. and Michael Smith, B.Pharm, M.R.Pharm.S., ND
- The Complete Kid's Allergy and Asthma Guide
  Edited by Dr. Milton Gold
- The Complete Natural Medicine Guide to Breast Cancer
  by Sat Dharam Kaur, ND
- The Complete Doctor's Stress Solution
  by Penny Kendall-Reed, MSc, ND and Dr. Stephen Reed, MD, FRCSC
- The Complete Doctor's Healthy Back Bible
  by Dr. Stephen Reed, MD and Penny Kendall-Reed, MSc, ND with Dr. Michael Ford, MD, FRCSC and Dr. Charles Gregory, MD, ChB, FRCP(C)
- Everyday Risks in Pregnancy & Breastfeeding
  by Dr. Gideon Koren, MD, FRCP(C), ND
- Help for Eating Disorders
  by Dr. Debra Katzman, MD, FRCP(C) and Dr. Leora Pinhas, MD

Also Available
from Robert Rose

125 best
**Vegetarian
Slow Cooker**
recipes

Judith Finlayson

For more great books see previous pages